DESERVED CRIMINAL SENTENCES

This book provides an accessible and systematic restatement of the desert model for criminal sentencing by one of its leading academic exponents. The desert model emphasises the degree of seriousness of the offender's crime in deciding the severity of his punishment, and has become increasingly influential in recent penal practice and scholarly debate. It explains why sentences should be based principally on crime-seriousness, and addresses, among other topics, how a desert-based penalty scheme can be constructed; how to gauge punishments' seriousness and penalties' severity; what weight should be given to an offender's previous convictions; how non-custodial sentences should be scaled; and what leeway there might be for taking other factors into account, such as an offender's need for treatment.

This volume will be of interest to all those working in penal theory and practice, criminal sentencing and the criminal law more generally.

Deserved Criminal Sentences

An Overview

Andreas von Hirsch

·HART·

OXFORD · LONDON · NEW YORK · NEW DELHI · SYDNEY

HART PUBLISHING

Bloomsbury Publishing Plc

Kemp House, Chawley Park, Cumnor Hill, Oxford, OX2 9PH, UK

HART PUBLISHING, the Hart/Stag logo, BLOOMSBURY and the Diana logo are
trademarks of Bloomsbury Publishing Plc

First published in Great Britain 2017

First published in hardback, 2017
Paperback edition, 2019

A catalogue record for this book is available from the British Library.

Library of Congress Cataloging-in-Publication Data

Names: Von Hirsch, Andrew, author.

Title: Deserved criminal sentences : an overview / Andreas von Hirsch.

Description: Oxford ; Portland, Oregon : Hart Publishing, an imprint of Bloomsbury
Publishing Plc, 2017. | Includes bibliographical references and index.

Identifiers: LCCN 2016037921 (print) | LCCN 2016038127 (ebook) | ISBN 9781509902668
(hardback : alk. paper) | ISBN 9781509902675 (Epub)

Subjects: LCSH: Punishment—Philosophy. | Sentences (Criminal procedure) | Proportionality in law.

Classification: LCC K5103 .V66 2017 (print) | LCC K5103 (ebook) | DDC 345/.0772—dc23

LC record available at https://lccn.loc.gov/2016037921

ISBN: HB: 978-1-50990-266-8
PB: 978-1-50993-005-0
ePDF: 978-1-50990-268-2
ePub: 978-1-50990-267-5

Typeset by Compuscript Ltd, Shannon

Preface

The subject matter of this book—the 'desert model' for criminal sentencing—is one on which I have written extensively over several decades. The model places primary emphasis, in deciding sentence, upon the degree of seriousness of the criminal conduct for which the defendant has been convicted—rather than (as traditional sentencing theories did) upon the expected impact of the sentence on the offender's likelihood of reoffending. The desert model attracted considerably more interest than I had anticipated when it was first proposed in the 1970s, and it continues to have widespread influence today.

This continuing interest in the desert model makes it desirable, I think, to provide a restatement of the model's main principles in concise, readily-readable form. No such up-to-date, easily available summary exists today. My previous accounts of the model are scattered through books and articles of varying accessibility, published at different times and in different places—with none of these having appeared since a decade ago. The aim of this volume, therefore, is to provide a restatement and explanation of the model's salient themes and of their conceptual basis.

Acknowledgements

In writing this book, I owe a debt of gratitude to a number of colleagues. I showed my initial draft to Andrew Ashworth and Julian Roberts, and their advice has been of great assistance. Julian also recommended a talented Young Israeli Scholar, Netanel Dagan, to assist me with references. Antonio Martins, my research assistant at the University of Frankfurt, ably helped in reviewing the arguments and in editing the manuscript's various drafts. Beto Gaedke, my secretary, deciphered the manuscript (and my numerous, scarcely-legible handwritten changes) with efficiency and patience.

In 2001 I published a comparable volume in Swedish,[1] when I held a visiting professorship in criminal law at the University of Uppsala. I had written an English-language draft for that volume, and my Uppsala colleague, Professor Nils Jareborg, generously took the time and effort to translate it into Swedish. I retained the English-language draft of the Swedish book in my files and made use of it a decade-and-a-half later in working on the present book.

I would also like to acknowledge the guidance, advice and support of many colleagues and friends with whom I have had extensive conversations over the years about the desert model, its justification, criteria and implications. They include: (i) in the US (where I taught at Rutgers University before the mid-1990s), David and Sheila Rothman, the late Harry Kalven, Marshall Cohen, Don M Gottfredson, Douglas Husak, the late Sheldon Messinger, Kay Knapp, John Kleinig, Judith Greene and Uma Narayan; (ii) in England (where I taught at Cambridge University from the mid-1990s to late 2000s), Andrew Ashworth, Anthony Bottoms, Julian V Roberts, Martin Wasik, Lucia Zedner and

---

[1] A von Hirsch, *Proportionalitet och Straffbestämning* (Uppsala, Iustus Förlag, 2001).

Antony Duff; (iii) in Gerrmany (where I have been teaching at the University of Frankfurt since 2008), Ulfrid Neumann, the late Winfried Hassemer, Wolfgang Frisch and Hans-Jörg Albrecht; and (iv) during my repeated visits to Uppsala, Sweden (since the early 1980s), Nils Jareborg, Dag Victor, Petter Asp, Karin Påle, Magnus Ulväng and Martin Borgeke.

My special thanks go to Professor Shin Matsuzawa of Waseda University Law School, Tokyo. He is undertaking a Japanese-language account of the desert model, and required an English-language overview of the theory. It was on the basis of his request I thus unearthed my draft English-language summary of a decade-and-a-half ago and revised and updated it for that purpose. It was he who also suggested publishing the English version, which has evolved into the present book.

Contents

Preface v

Acknowledgements vii

1. Introduction: The Emergence of the Proportionate
   Sentence 1
   1.1 The Origins of the Desert Model 1
   1.2 Proportionality-based Sentencing: The Example
       of Sweden's Sentencing Scheme 4
   1.3 Attractions of the Proportionate Sentence 7
   1.4 Prevention-based Sentencing as a
       Workable Alternative? 8
   1.5 Ethical Presuppositions of the
       Desert Rationale 11
   1.6 Topics Addressed in this Volume 13

2. Sentence Proportionality Sketched Briefly 17
   2.1 Censure and Penal Desert 17
   2.2 The Rationale for Proportionality 20
   2.3 Proportionality as 'Limiting' or 'Determining'? 21
   2.4 Gauging Crimes' Seriousness and
       Punishments' Severity 23
   2.5 Role of Previous Criminal Convictions 24
   2.6 Inclusion of Crime-control Aims? 25
   2.7 Desert and Increased Penal Severity? 27

3. Why Should the Criminal Sanction Exist? 29
   3.1 Varieties of Desert Theories 29
   3.2 Censure-Based Justifications for Punishment 31
   3.3 Why the Censure in Punishment? 32
   3.4 Why the Hard Treatment in Punishment? 36
   3.5 The Relation between the Two Elements 39

4. Why Punish Proportionately? 45
   4.1 Beccaria and Bentham's Deterrence Argument 46

4.2   Positive General Prevention: The
Inhibition-reinforcement Argument 47
4.3   The Argument from Censure...49
4.4   The Censure Argument Stated More Fully.............................50

5.   Ordinal and Cardinal Proportionality...55
5.1   Ordinal Proportionality...56
5.2   The Sub-requirements of Ordinal Proportionality:
Parity and Rank-ordering...58
5.3   How Much Does Ordinal Proportionality Constrain
Reliance on Crime-prevention Concerns?.............................58
5.4   Cardinal Magnitude and the Fixing of the
Penalty System's Anchoring Points..59
5.5   How Much Guidance Regarding Anchoring of
the Penalty Structure?...60

6.   Seriousness, Severity and the Living-standard................................63
6.1   Gauging Crimes' Seriousness...63
6.2   Gauging Punishments' Severity..67

7.   The Role of Previous Convictions...71
7.1   Explanations Directed to the Present Act...............................73
7.2   Explanations Directed to the Criminal Career......................74
7.3   An Alternative Account: 'Tolerance' and
the Prior Record...75
7.4   Multiple Previous Offending?..79
7.5   The Institutional and Social Context......................................80
7.6   An Illustration: Sweden's Treatment
of Reoffending...82
7.7   Seriousness and Number of Previous
Convictions...84

8.   Proportionate Non-custodial Sanctions..87
8.1   Basic Elements of the Model..87
8.2   Interchanges: Equivalent Penal Bite.......................................89
8.3   Back-up Sanctions for Breach of Conditions.......................93

9.   A 'Modified' Desert Model?..97
9.1   Exceptional Departures...98
9.2   'Range Models'..103
9.2a   'Limiting Retributivism'...103
9.2b   A 'Modified' Desert Model..104

10. The Politics of the Desert Model 107
     10.1 The Desert Model's Political Pedigree 107
     10.2 Limiting Severity: Desert vs Penal
           Utilitarianism 111
     10.3 Proportionality and Increased Severity? 115
     10.4 'Law and Order' Strategies 118
     10.5 Arguments about 'Underlying Ills' 122
     10.6 The 'Vacuousness' Argument 125

11. Proportionate Sentences for Juveniles 127
     11.1 Introduction 127
     11.2 Culpability 129
           11.2a Cognitive Factors 130
           11.2b Volitional Controls 133
           11.2c Youth 'Discount' or Individual
                   Assessment? 134
     11.3 Punitive Bite 135
     11.4 A Special 'Tolerance' for Juveniles? 137

Appendix: The Desert Model's Evolution—A Brief
     Chronology 143

Bibliography 151
Index 161

1

Introduction: The Emergence of the Proportionate Sentence

IN THIS VOLUME, I wish to provide an overview of a theory of criminal sentencing that emphasises the degree of seriousness of a convicted offender's criminal conduct, in deciding the severity of his punishment. This approach calls for a supporting rationale, and the rationale that I address herein is often referred to (especially in English-language discussion) as the 'desert model'. 'Desert', literally is simply that which is deserved, and a variety of reasons (including traditional retributive conceptions) might be offered concerning how much punishment offenders deserve. The 'desert model' which I shall be defending here, however, is a newer, rather than the traditional account; it is one which has had considerable influence in contemporary penology, and which I have been instrumental in developing over recent decades.

Stated briefly, this desert model contains two main elements. The first is a criterion for deciding the severity of sentences, to wit: the principle of *proportionality*, according to which a sentence's severity should be made fairly proportionate to the seriousness of the defendant's criminal conduct. The second is a suggested conceptual basis for this principle: one that emphasises punishment's role of conveying *censure* or disapprobation of a convicted person for his or her criminal misconduct.

1.1 THE ORIGINS OF THE DESERT MODEL

The groundwork for the desert perspective for sentencing was laid in the Anglo-American post-World War literature of analytical moral philosophy. This writing supplied a principled critique of purely instrumental ways of thinking about social and penal issues, suggesting how these were capable of sacrificing individual rights in order to serve collective societal interests.[1] The philosophical literature also began exploring the notion of desert, suggesting how it constitutes an important part of ordinary moral judgements.[2]

The movement towards the modern proportionality-based conception of sentencing began in 1971, with the publication of the Quaker-sponsored American Friends Service Committee report, *Struggle for Justice* (1972).[3] The report recommended moderate, proportionate punishments, and opposed deciding sentence-severity on predictive or rehabilitative grounds. The Friends Committee report did not rely explicitly on the idea of desert as the basis for its proposals; that was left to subsequent writings, including the Australian philosopher John Kleinig's *Punishment and Desert* (1973),[4] and my own *Doing Justice: The Choice of Punishments* (1976).[5] A number of British, American, Scandinavian, and German penologists have since contributed to this discussion.[6] The present volume summarises this literature, including my subsequent writings.[7]

---

[1] See, eg, Bernard Williams, 'A Critique of Utilitarianism' in JJC Smart and B Williams (eds), *Utilitarianism: For and Against* (Cambridge, Cambridge University Press, 1973).

[2] KG Armstrong, 'The Retributivist Hits Back' (1961) *Mind* 70, 471; H Morris, 'Persons and Punishments' (1968) *Monist* 52, 475.

[3] American Friends Service Committee, *Struggle for Justice* (New York, Hill and Wang, 1972).

[4] J Kleinig, *Punishment and Desert* (The Hague, Nijhoff, 1973).

[5] A von Hirsch, *Doing Justice: The Choice of Punishments* (New York, Hill and Wang, 1976; reprinted 1986 (Boston, Northeastern University Press)).

[6] See references in this chapter below—most notably, A Ashworth, *Sentencing and Criminal Justice*, 6th edn (Cambridge, Cambridge University Press, 2015) Chs 4–6.

[7] Particularly, A von Hirsch, *Past or Future Crimes: Deservedness and Dangerousness in the Sentencing of Criminals* (New Brunswick, New Jersey, Rutgers University Press, 1985; UK edn 1986 (Manchester, Manchester University Press)); A von Hirsch, *Censure and Sanctions* (Oxford, Oxford University Press, 1993); A von Hirsch and A Ashworth, *Proportionate Sentencing: Exploring the Principles* (Oxford, Oxford University Press, 2005); and A von Hirsch, 'Proportionality and the Progressive Loss of Mitigation: Some Further Reflections' in A von Hirsch and JV Roberts (eds), *Previous Convictions at Sentencing: Theoretical and Applied Perspectives* (Oxford, Hart Publishing, 2010) Ch 1. For a different version of desert theory based on the notion of punishment as penance, see RA Duff, *Trials and Punishments* (Cambridge, Cambridge University Press, 1986); RA Duff, *Punishment, Communication, and Community* (New York, Oxford University Press, 2001). For a critique of Duff's version, see von Hirsch and Ashworth 2005, Ch 7.

The notion of deserved sentences has had a curious history in modern penological theory, of first being virtually ignored, and then suddenly becoming quite influential. Judges, as a matter of practice, have long based their sentences to a considerable extent upon the degree of seriousness of defendants' crimes. Philosophers, for centuries, have debated retribution as a rationale for punishment. In sentencing theory during the first six decades of the twentieth century, however, the idea of desert went into eclipse; it came either to be ignored, or else dismissed as obsolete, vindictive or obscure.

Once the conception of desert was reintroduced in the sentencing debate in the 1970s, however, it began to be argued that, far from being obsolete, desert should be treated as the central conception of justice in sentencing. The idea of the deserved, proportionate sentence has by now taken a substantial role in academic penological discussion.[8] The idea has also influenced sentencing-reform efforts in a number of jurisdictions, including some American states; Finland and Sweden among the Nordic countries; England;[9] and, most recently, Israel.[10] The idea has also become influential in academic debate over sentencing throughout Western Europe and North America.

---

[8] For a recent summary and analysis of these developments, see Ashworth 2015, Ch 4. For a strongly-worded recent critique of the desert model, however, see N Lacey and H Pickard (2015), 'The Chimera of Proportionality: Institutionalising Limits on Punishment in Contemporary Social and Political Systems' (2015) *Modern Law Review* 78, 216.

[9] In 2003, the UK Parliament established a Sentencing Guidelines Council consisting of senior judges, legal scholars and criminologists, to provide explicit guidance for sentencing decisions. In the following year, that body promulgated, as a major Guideline, an' overarching principle' relying substantially on conceptions of desert. This norm provides that a sentencing court 'is required to pass a sentence that is commensurate with the seriousness of the offence' (with offence-seriousness to be determined by the harm or risk caused by the offence and by the degree of culpability of the offender in committing it). The assessment of the crime's seriousness, the Guideline further states, should provide indication of whether a custodial, community or other sentence would be appropriate. See, Sentencing Guidelines Council (England and Wales), *Overarching Principles: Seriousness* (London, Sentencing Guidelines Council, 2004); and for fuller discussion, Ashworth 2015, Ch 4.

[10] For a description and analysis of Israel's new desert-oriented sentencing statute, see JV Roberts and O Gazal-Ayal, 'Statutory Sentencing Reform in Israel: Exploring the Sentencing Law of 2012' (2013) *Israel Law Review* 46, 455.

The developing literature on desert addressed two principal objections that had been made to traditional retributive notions. One objection was that deserved punishment was incomprehensible, that it rested on obscure 'metaphysical' notions such as that of requiting evil for evil. Modern desert theorists provided a more straightforward account, however, grounded in the familiar logic of everyday ethical discourse. Punishment, they pointed out, is a *blaming* institution. The difference, for example, between a fine and a civil monetary sanction lies generally in the fact that the former conveys disapprobation or censure of the actor for his criminal acts, whereas the latter does not.

Fairness requires, therefore, that penalties be allocated consistently with their censuring implications. Thus, the severity of the punishment (and thereby the degree of disapprobation visited on the actor) should reflect the degree of blameworthiness (that is, the seriousness), of the defendant's criminal conduct. Disproportionate or disparate punishments are unjust, not because they fail to properly requite suffering with suffering, but because they treat offenders as more or less worthy of penal disapprobation than the reprehensibleness of their conduct warrants.

The other objection was to the seeming harshness of retributive punishment, to its apparent talionic character as exaction of an 'eye for an eye'. Modern desert theorists' response has been that desert definitively does not demand visitation of suffering equal to the harm done by criminal acts to their victims. What is required, instead, is that punishments be *proportionate* to the seriousness of the defendant's criminal conduct. Proportionate punishments can be levied without increasing—indeed, while substantially decreasing—prevailing severity levels, as long as penalties are ordered to reflect crimes' comparative degree of blameworthiness.[11]

1.2 PROPORTIONALITY-BASED SENTENCING: THE EXAMPLE OF SWEDEN'S SENTENCING SCHEME

In the decades after the Second World War, Sweden became internationally noted for its interest in penal rehabilitation. Actually, that nation did not go as far as foreign observers supposed. Indeterminate

---

[11] See more fully, chs 5 and 10 below.

treatment-based sentences were used mainly for special offender categories—such as youthful offenders and habitual criminals. The Swedish Penal Code did not, indeed, have much to say on choice of sentence. The Code did refer to rehabilitation and deterrence in general terms, but gave scant guidance on how such aims should be implemented by the courts in their sentencing decisions.

During the late 1970s, Sweden experienced growing disenchantment with its treatment-based law and conceptions of sentencing. The existing Penal Code provisions, it was felt, gave insufficient guidance to courts for choosing the sanction. It also began to be recognised that only a limited capacity exists for sentences to achieve much rehabilitative effect. Questions were raised further about the fairness of basing sanctions on a defendant's supposed responsiveness to treatment or on his likelihood of future offending. There developed new interest in the idea of sentence-proportionality; in penal sanctions that would comport fairly with the degree of seriousness of defendants' criminal acts.

This new thinking received considerable stimulus with the publication in 1977 of a Swedish government research committee's report, *A New Penal System*.[12] This report, drafted by a working party of judges and penologists, emphasised ideas of proportionate sentences, and of limiting sentencing discretion. Such themes, then referred to as 'neoclassical', were echoed in an influential essay collection, *Punishment and Justice*, that appeared a few years later, in 1980.[13]

The Swedish reformers' first success was their campaign to abolish the indeterminate sentence. We have, they asserted, neither the capacity to identify persons who are long-term risks with sufficient accuracy, nor the ability to treat such persons which this measure presupposed. Indeterminate confinement for youthful offenders was eliminated in 1979, and long-term 'internment' for repeat adult offenders was eliminated two years later.

The next and crucial step was to address the Penal Code's general provisions concerning sentencing. In 1979, the Swedish Minister of Justice appointed an advisory committee of judges, jurists, and criminologists—the 'Fängelsestraffkommittén'—whose report

---

[12] Brottsförebyggande rådet, *Nytt Strafsystem: Idéer och Förslag* (Stockholm, Brottsförebyggande rådet, 1977).

[13] S Heckscher et al (eds), *Straff och rättfärdighet: Ny nordisk debatt* (Stockolm, Norstedts, 1980).

appeared a decade later, in 1986.[14] The report, among its various recommendations, proposed lowering the statutory maximum sentences
for many crimes, expanding the system of unit-fines (that is, fines measured by fractions of the defendant's earnings), and changing the rules
on parole release. Its most notable proposal, however, concerned the
principles governing the choice of sentence. The Committee proposed
two wholly new chapters of the Penal Code dealing with sentencing.
These were enacted by Sweden's legislature in 1988 as Chapters 29 and
30 of the Penal Code, and took effect in the following year.

These new provisions were designed to emphasise proportionality
of sentence. They make the severity of the sentence depend primarily on the 'penal value' (ie, the seriousness) of the defendant's crime.[15]
Penal value, under the law, should be determined by the degree of
harmfulness of the criminal conduct, and by the offender's degree
of culpability in committing it.[16] Aggravating and mitigating circumstances are listed in the statute,[17] and these generally refer to situations
of specially heightened or reduced harmfulness or culpability of the
defendant's conduct. Imprisonment may be used chiefly in two kinds
of situations: when the penal value (seriousness) of the criminal conduct is high; and when the penal value is in the intermediate range, but
the offender has accumulated a significant record of previous convictions. The structure of the law has remained essentially the same since
the statute's enactment in 1988.

The Swedish law was influenced considerably by the Finnish sentencing statute,[18] which was enacted in 1976, more than a decade before
Sweden' s law. The sentence, according to the Finnish law, should be in
'just proportion' to the harmfulness of the conduct and the culpability
of the offender as expressed through the conduct. Predictive and rehabilitative concerns were largely to be excluded in deciding the severity
of the sentence. The Finnish law spells out the steps in determining the

---

[14] Fängelsestraffkommittén, *Påföljd för Brott* (Stockholm, Stadens Offentlige
Utredingar, 1986) 14.

[15] Swedish Penal Code, chs 29 and 30.

[16] Swedish Penal Code, Ch 29, s 1.

[17] Swedish Penal Code, Ch 29, ss 2 and 3.

[18] The statute is set forth in the Finnish Penal Code, Ch 6. For an analysis of
the law, see T Lappi-Seppälä, 'Penal Policy in Scandinavia' in M Tonry (ed), *Crime,
Punishment, and Politics in a Comparative Perspective. Crime and Justice* (Chicago, Chicago
University Press, 2007) vol 36.

proportionate sentence less fully than the Swedish law, but the emphasis on proportionality is comparable.

1.3 ATTRACTIONS OF THE PROPORTIONATE SENTENCE

If proportionalism in sentencing has had such recent influence, what has made it attractive? One attraction has been that it offers better practical guidance: it explicitly provides a way of deciding approximately how much punishment a convicted defendant should receive. Traditional preventively oriented approaches largely failed to offer such guidance. The Swedish Penal Code before 1989, for example, provided that the sentence should be determined so as to promote general obedience to law, and foster the defendant's rehabilitation.[19] But it was far from clear how courts were to achieve these aims, especially given the paucity of effective treatments, and the tenuous connection between promoting general law-abidingness and the sentence imposed in any particular case.

A desert-based sentencing model is capable of giving sentencing judges better guidance: it can suggest what offence and offender characteristics should be given primacy, and help decide what these factors' comparative emphasis should be in deciding sentences. It points to the seriousness of the offence as the primary determinant in the choice of sentence. It offers principles for ranking and comparing penalties, namely, the principles of ordinal proportionality discussed below (Chapter 5). It indicates how much weight (namely, only limited weight) should be given to the offender's previous convictions (Chapter 7).

Another attraction of a proportionalist approach has been its emphasis on fairness. Traditional preventively-oriented sentencing theories, even when they purported to be humane, focused chiefly on instrumental concerns: which sentencing strategy can better protect *us* from the depredations of *them*, the potential criminals. Such instrumentalism threaten unjust results: if the chief aim is prevention, why not do whatever seems to work for the purpose? Even during the heyday of penal rehabilitationism, when the rehabilitative sentence was supposed to foster the defendant's interests as well as to protect the public, this potential for unfairness was manifest—as was evident in the use of

---

[19] See former Swedish Penal Code (1968), Ch 1, s 7.

long indeterminate confinements for the purpose of treatment. When preventive goals shift from rehabilitation to deterrence and incapacitation, the potential oppressiveness of preventively-oriented sentencing becomes still more apparent: in the possibility, for example, of disproportionately long prison sentences to achieve such ends.

A desert rationale, and the principle of proportionality it supports, gives notions of justice the central role in determining sentence. Proportionality of sentence, on this perspective, rests on the idea that the penal censure expressed through the sanction should fairly reflect the degree of reprehensibility of the defendant's criminal conduct—that is, its degree of harmfulness and culpability (see Chapter 4). This viewpoint helps to deal with the tension over whether penal policy should favour societal interests or the interests of offenders. In desert theory, the societal interest is expressed in the recognition that typical crimes (eg, those of force and fraud) are wrongs, for which public condemnation through the criminal sanction is due. The individual's interest is protected through his entitlement to no severer punishment than the degree of blameworthiness that his conduct warrants, even if a harsher sentence might possibly have greater preventive effects.

Desert-based punishment has been characterised by some critics as a return to traditional talionic notions of 'an eye for an eye'. That emphatically is not so. The desert rationale rests on the idea of a *proportion* rather than harm-for-harm equivalence: penalties need not visit as much suffering as the harm done by offences to their victims. A substantial deflation in overall penalty levels is permissible—indeed, is desirable—so long as penalties are graded in the order of crimes' seriousness (see further, Chapter 5).

1.4 PREVENTION-BASED SENTENCING AS A WORKABLE ALTERNATIVE?

An alternative to proportionate sentencing might be preventively-oriented approaches, according to which sentences would be decided so as to maximise or optimise deterrent, rehabilitative, or incapacitative effects. When proportionalism emerged in the 1970s, however, it was against a background of growing scepticism about the workability and fairness of such preventively-oriented sentencing conceptions. Such scepticism, I think, remains warranted today.[20]

An important reason why the institution of the criminal sanction should exist at all is that it helps prevent crime. The desert model, as is suggested in the ensuing chapters, relies upon crime-prevention along with censure of criminal behaviour as the twin (and intertwined) justifications for the existence of a system of punishment (see Chapter 3). But sentencing policy addresses not whether punishment should exist, but *how much* offenders convicted of various kinds of crimes should be punished. A chiefly crime-preventative sentencing policy would require us to have adequate knowledge of *marginal* preventive effects: how much more criminality may be prevented if a severer sentence X is imposed rather than a more lenient one, Y. Such knowledge is largely non-existent.

Consider rehabilitation. It was fashionable for a time among some American criminologists to assert that 'nothing works'—that rehabilitative programmes virtually never succeed in reducing offender recidivism.[21] That is overstated, for some successes have been reported for certain types of treatment directed at specified types of offenders.[22] No general 'cure' is known, however, for routine cases of (say) car theft, burglary, or robbery. Treatment, although it may have a modest role to play, cannot serve as the chief underpinning of sentencing theory and policy.[23]

Consider, next, general deterrence. General-deterrent effects can be discerned when previously unpunished conduct is made punishable: a noted British example being the criminalisation of drinking and driving in the

---

[20] For a recent discussion of the role of crime-prevention aims in sentencing theory, see A Ashworth and L Zedner, *Preventive Justice* (New York, Oxford University Press, 2014).

[21] Particularly, R Martinson, 'What Works?—Questions and Answers about Prison Reform' (1974) *Public Interest* 35, 25.

[22] See, eg, AE Bottoms and A von Hirsch, 'The Crime-Preventive Impact of Penal Sanctions' in P Cane and HM Kritzer (eds), *The Oxford Handbook of Empirical Legal Studies* (Oxford, Oxford University Press, 2010) 107–13.

[23] For an optimistic account of the prospects of successful treatment strategies, however, see FT Cullen and KE Gilbert (2012), *Reaffirming Rehabilitation*, 2nd edn (London, Routledge, 2012); see also C Slobogin, 'Prevention as the Primary Goal of Sentencing: The Modern Case for Interdeterminate Dispositions in Criminal Cases' (2011) *San Diego Law Review* 48, 1127.

1960s. Citizens who are law-abiding by inclination tend to avoid such conduct when it becomes prohibited and punishable. But in sentencing policy, the issue is not such initial deterrence, but rather *marginal* deterrence: how much *extra* prevention is achieved through alteration of penalty levels for already-punishable conduct. The kind of marginal preventive effects that are relevant here thus are not 'certainty' effects (the extra deterrence achieved by increasing the likelihood of apprehension and conviction), but 'severity' effects—namely the marginal deterrence achieved by increasing the onerousness of punishment for those convicted.

While there is some tentative evidence that 'certainty' may affect crime rates, the evidence for 'severity' effects is much weaker. Recent deterrence research, mirroring earlier studies, fails to disclose significant and consistent associations between severity levels (such as duration of imprisonment) and crime rates.[24] Little also is known about the extent to which offenders inform themselves about changes in penalty levels. The existing data simply does not provide the basis for valid inferences about whether and how much of punishments' severities would need to be determined in order to achieve significantly increased deterrent effects.[25]

What about incapacitation? It has been possible, for many years already, to make rough-and-ready forecasts about which convicted offenders would be more likely to return to crime. That might seem to offer a practical alternative to proportionality-based sentencing: namely, calibrating sentences according to offenders' apparent risk of recidivism. Schemes of this kind have been proposed, most notably, in the 'selective incapacitation' schemes promoted by some conservative American penologists in the early 1980s.[26] Crime prevention, however,

---

[24] Bottoms and von Hirsch 2010, Ch 4, 98–106.

[25] Ibid; CM Webster and AN Doob, 'Searching for Sasquatch: Deterrence of Crime through Sentence Severity' in J Petersilia and KR Reitz (eds), *The Oxford Handbook of Sentencing and Corrections* (New York, Oxford University Press, 2012); B Jacobs and A Piquero, 'Boundary-Crossing in Perceptual Deterrence' (2013) *International Journal of Offender Therapy and Comparative Criminology* 57, 792; R Apel, 'Sanctions, Perceptions, and Crime: Implications for Criminal Deterrence' (2013) *Journal of Quantitative Criminology* 29, 67.

[26] PW Greenwood, *Selective Incapacitation* (Santa Monica, California, RAND Corporation, 1982).; JQ Wilson, *Thinking about Crime*, revised edn (New York, Basic Books, 1983) Ch 8; see also, Virginia's prediction-based sentencing guidelines, discussed in RS Frase, *Just Sentencing: Principles and Procedures for a Workable System* (New York, Oxford University Press, 2013) 166.

is ultimately concerned with reducing *net* risks of victimisation. It is scarcely reassuring citizens that certain convicted robbers would be prevented from robbing again, if the general likelihood of citizens being victimised by other robbers remained unchanged.

Notwithstanding claims by some of its proponents, selective incapacitation has little apparent effectiveness when judged by this norm of net impact on crime rates. Enthusiasm for selective incapacitation began to wane with the publication of a 1986 (US) National Academy of Sciences report, suggesting how small that preventive impact was likely to be.[27]

Beyond these problems of effectiveness, which would be difficult to remedy, prevention-based sentencing strategies also suffer from a fairness deficit: they result in sentences that fail to comport with the censuring implications of punishment. Imposing a more severe punishment on an offender involves blaming him more. On the proportionalist approach, this is warranted only when his criminal conduct has been worse—ie, more blameworthy. Preventively-based sentencing theories, however, make the quantum of the sentence depend largely on ulterior factors: the offender's potential responsiveness to treatment, the possible impact of his sentence on others' inclination to offend, or various other facts about the offender that might predict his future offending. It is such concerns about justice that, fundamentally, militate in favour of proportionalist sentencing.[28]

1.5 ETHICAL PRESUPPOSITIONS OF THE DESERT RATIONALE

The proportionalist sentencing rationale outlined in this book rests on certain ethical presuppositions. It is worth spelling these out.

---

[27] National Academy of Sciences, Panel on Research on Criminal Careers, 'Criminal Careers and "Career Criminals"' (edited by A Blumstein, J Cohen, J Roth and C Visher) (Washington DC, National Academies of Sciences Press, 1986) Vol 1; see also von Hirsch 1985, Chs 9–12; and, recently, MB Perez and R Argueta, 'Selective Incapacitation' in J Albanese (ed), *The Encyclopedia of Criminology and Criminal Justice* (New Jersey, Wiley, 2014); see also Bottoms and von Hirsch 2010, 113–20.

[28] Predictive sentencing has further ethical deficiencies—for example, concerning misclassification: a substantial number of those classified as bad risks (and hence given severer sentences) would not actually be found to reoffend were they to remain at liberty. See von Hirsch 1985, Chs 9 and 11.

First, it is assumed that, in sentencing, the requirements of justice ought substantially to constrain the pursuit of crime prevention. That assumption represents a departure from traditional thinking about sentencing policy. It had commonly been supposed that the requirements of justice had largely been satisfied once the offender was fairly tried and convicted. Thereafter, attention was supposed to turn to crime prevention; and penologists were chiefly concerned with which preventive strategies promoted public safety best.

This assumption of the primacy of justice alters the focus of sentencing theory. A conception of sentencing cannot be justified merely by pointing to its possible crime-preventive utility: it is necessary to consider whether such a scheme would be just, and why so. Proportionality of sentence is defended in this volume chiefly on the basis that it constitutes a *fair* way of deciding how much to punish.

Second, it is assumed that the penal response ought to take a form that treats the convicted offender as a *moral agent*—that is, as a person capable of reflecting upon the appropriateness of his actions. The desert model's emphasis on censure as the basis for proportionality requirements (see, especially, Chapter 4) is premised on punishment's role in addressing a potential actor's sense of right or wrong, and on giving him the opportunity to respond as a moral agent capable of evaluating the propriety of his actions. Penal responses that merely seek to restrain or intimidate the actor into compliance, or which penalise the offender chiefly in order to alter the behaviour of others, are thus problematic.

Third, it is assumed that the state should exercise self-restraint in intervening in convicted offenders' lives. In setting sentencing policy, the state should have the burden of explaining why proposed levels of punitiveness, rather than lesser ones, are called for. Severe penalties should bear an especially heavy burden of justification.

Finally, it is assumed that sentencing policy should be governed by principles of rule of law. The legal regulations governing choice of sentence should explicitly prescribe what punishment-norms should apply in making that choice. Those norms may be stated in general terms, and give scope for interpretation and a reasonable margin of discretion in individual cases. But purely or primarily discretionary sentencing approaches, which leave it up to individual sentencing judges to decide what sentencing aims to pursue and how much punishment to impose, should have no place in a penal system that is governed by the rule of law.

1.6 TOPICS ADDRESSED IN THIS VOLUME

This book attempts to present a compact but systematic account of the desert model. A number of its themes are drawn from Andrew Ashworth's and my 2005 volume, *Proportionate Sentencing*,[29] which constitutes our most recent extended discussion of that rationale. However, the present volume also reflects subsequent thinking of mine on some issues.

The immediately-succeeding chapter (Chapter 2) describes the main tenets of desert theory, that is, of a proportionalist sentencing perspective. It is designed to give the reader a sense of this sentencing conception as a whole, and thus make the ensuing discussions of particular topics more readily comprehensible.

The ensuing six chapters address various aspects of the proportionalist sentencing rationale more fully. They cover the following topics:

— The rationale for the existence of the criminal sanction (Chapter 3). This discussion pays particular attention to the role of and justification for penal censure in punishment.
— The rationale for the principle of proportionality of sentence (Chapter 4). Proportionality seems to be a common-sense requirement of justice in punishing, but its supporting reasons need explicit elucidation. The proposed rationale links proportionality to the idea of penal censure.
— The character of proportionality requirements (Chapter 5). Even when proportionality of sentence is assumed to be a requirement of justice, the question remains of how and how much that principle helps to guide the choice of sentence. Does the principle merely suggest broad outer limits on the permissible sanction, within which a particular offender's sentence may be chosen on ulterior (particularly, crime-prevention) grounds? Or does it impose more detailed requirements on the ranking and scaling of penalties? It will be argued that the principle calls for the latter: for *ordinal* proportionality constraints that impose definite requirements regarding the comparative ordering of punishments. However, the conception of penal desert provides less guidance about the overall

---

[29] von Hirsch and Ashworth 2005.

degree of punitiveness or leniency of the penalty system—although certain principles can be identified, that point toward maintaining moderate levels of punishment.

— Gauging the seriousness of crimes and assessing the severity of punishments (Chapter 6). The proportionality-principle requires that the *seriousness* of crimes should govern the *severity* of punishment. This raises the question of how crime-seriousness and punishment- severity, respectively, are to be assessed. The chapter suggests using the notion of the 'living standard' to judge the harm-component in crime seriousness, and also for assessing the comparative severities of various sanctions.

— The weight to be given to previous convictions in determining sentence (Chapter 7). Most sentencing systems adjust an offender's sentence upward when he has a record of previous convictions. On an incapacitative theory of sentencing, this seems simple enough: an offender's previous criminal record is a useful predictor of recidivism. But on a desert rationale, the question seems more perplexing. Since the offender has been punished already for his previous misdeed, how can his record of previous offending bear on how much he deserves for his current offence? The chapter will argue in favour of a limited adjustment in the sentence on account of an offender's prior convictions. It will also offer a 'tolerance theory', designed to suggest why such an adjustment comports with conceptions of penal desert.

— Proportionate non-custodial penalties (Chapter 8). Prison sentences can be compared with one another by reference to their duration. Non-custodial sanctions seem to be more difficult to scale, however, because they may impinge upon differing interests. How, for example, can the severity of a fine (which affects the defendant's financial resources) be compared with that of probation (which affects his freedom of movement)? The chapter will sketch a model for comparing and scaling non- custodial penalties.

— A 'modified' desert model will next be considered (Chapter 9). This will address schemes which rely principally on desert-based considerations; but nevertheless permit a limited derogation from proportionality constraints in order to provide some added scope for crime-preventive or other aims.

— The ensuing chapter will address political conceptions underlying sentencing (Chapter 10). It will describe the basic political
presuppositions of the desert model (broadly liberal, in the civil-
liberties sense of that term); the influence of a proportionalist sentencing rationale on trends toward greater or less severity; and the
nature (and hazards) of 'law and order' pressures on sentencing.
— The applicability of the desert model to juvenile justice will finally
be addressed (Chapter 11). Traditionally, juvenile justice has been
the area where rehabilitative perspectives have been particularly
dominant. However, desert theorists have begun to sketch how
desert considerations may be made applicable to juveniles; and
what adjustment from an adult desert model would be needed for
that purpose.

One important issue I shall not address in detail in this volume is that
of guidance or guidelines for sentencing. The traditional rehabilitative
sentencing ethos supported granting individual judges wide discretion
regarding the aims which a sentence was supposed to achieve. That
approach, however, permitted wide sentencing disparities, as individual
judges relied on differing reasons for deciding similar cases.

When the desert model emerged in the 1970s, its advocates (including myself) favoured explicit sentencing guidance to help assure that
desert rationale would be applied, and applied consistently, in judges'
sentencing decisions.[30] In the ensuing American discussion, the proposed guidance tended to take the form of numerical guidelines: that is,
numerical tables showing recommended sentences of various degrees
of onerousness, depending on the seriousness of the offender's
offence, and on the frequency and gravity of his previous convictions.
Minnesota's sentencing guidelines, one of the first guidance schemes
influenced by desert theory, took that form.[31] In Europe, however,
there was scant interest in such numerical schemes. Guidance was
achieved (in Sweden and Finland, for example) through explicit, legis-
latively-adopted guiding principles, to be applied in individual cases by

[30] See, eg von Hirsch 1976, Ch 12.
[31] See, eg A von Hirsch, K Knapp and M Tonry, *The Sentencing Commission and its
Guidelines* (Boston, Northeastern University Press, 1987); Frase 2013, Ch 3.

the courts.[32] An extensive literature has developed on differing forms of guidance and their relative merits.[33]

My reason for omitting detailed discussion of this topic of various techniques of sentencing guidance from this book is that I have come to think that differing modes of guidance may be suitable, depending on the history, traditions and structure of sentencing system in various jurisdictions. The issue is also of a more technical nature than would be appropriate here. Those interested in this topic may consult the extensive literature that has been developed on the topic.[34]

* * *

To provide a compact account of the desert model, this book presents it as a unified theory. However, the model was developed over an extended period, through the work of a number of contributors. The Appendix to this volume sketches how the theory has developed, and who have contributed to it.

---

[32] For a description of Sweden's approach, see eg, N Jareborg, 'The Swedish Sentencing Reform' in C Clarkson and R Morgan (eds), *The Politics of Sentencing Reform* (Oxford, Oxford University Press, 1995). England's sentencing guidelines take the form of sentencing principles formulated by a judicial regulatory body, the Sentencing Guidelines Council; see A Ashworth and JV Roberts (eds), *Sentencing Guidelines: Exploring the English Model* (Oxford, Oxford University Press, 2013).

[33] Such discussion has been led by Michael Tonry in the US; by Andrew Ashworth, Julian Roberts and Martin Wasik in the UK; and by Nils Jareborg, Dag Victor and Martin Borgeke in Sweden, and by Tapio Lappi-Seppälä in Finland. For some of the literature, see eg, von Hirsch, Knapp and Tonry 1987; M Wasik and K Pease (eds), *Sentencing Reform: Guidance or Guidelines?* (Manchester, Manchester University Press, 1987); A Ashworth, 'Sentencing Guidelines and the Sentencing Council' (2010) *Criminal Law Review* 389; Ashworth and Roberts 2013; and Frase 2013.

[34] Ibid.

2

Sentence Proportionality Sketched Briefly

I N THIS CHAPTER, I shall provide an outline of the desert model's basic tenets and its supporting rationale. Subsequent chapters will then examine such issues more fully.

2.1 CENSURE AND PENAL DESERT

There have been a variety of retributive or desert-based accounts of punishment, ranging from intuitionist theories,[1] to talionic notions of requiting evil for evil, to conceptions that view punishment as taking away the 'unjust advantage' which the offender obtains by choosing to offend.[2] The desert-based conception discussed in this volume, however, relies on a different account: one emphasising the communicative features of punishment.

The criminal sanction censures: punishing consists of doing something unpleasant to someone, because he has committed a wrong, under circumstances and in a manner that conveys disapprobation of the person for his wrongdoing. Treating the offender as a wrongdoer is central to the idea of punishment. The difference between a tax and a fine, for example, does not rest in the material deprivation imposed—which is money in both cases. It consists, rather, in the fact

---

[1] See eg M Moore, *Placing Blame: A General Theory of Criminal Law* (Oxford, Clarendon Press, 1997) Chs 3 and 4.
[2] See M Davis, 'How to Make the Punishment Fit the Crime' (1983) *Ethics* 93, 726 and for a critique of Davis's theory, A von Hirsch, *Censure and Sanctions* (Oxford, Oxford University Press, 1993) 7–8.

that with a fine, money is taken in a manner that visits the offender with disapprobation; whereas with a tax, no disapproval is necessarily implied.[3]

A sanction that treats the conduct as wrong—that is, not a 'neutral' sanction—has two important normative functions that are not reducible to crime prevention.[4] One is to recognise the importance of the rights that have been infringed. The censure in punishment conveys to victims the acknowledgment that they are *wronged* by criminal conduct, that rights to which they properly are entitled have been intruded upon. The other (and, still more important) role of censure is that of addressing the offender as a moral agent. A human actor, this communicative perspective suggests, should be treated as a person capable (unless mentally disabled) of evaluating the propriety of his conduct. A response to criminal wrongdoing that involves censure gives the offender the opportunity to respond in ways that are appropriate for an agent capable of moral deliberation: to recognise the wrongfulness of the action and to make efforts to desist in future—or else to try to offer reasons why his conduct was not actually wrong. What a purely 'neutral' sanction not embodying blame would deny (even if no less effective in preventing crime) is precisely this recognition of the person's status as a moral agent. A neutral sanction would treat offenders and potential offenders much as dangerous beasts—as creatures which need merely to be restrained or intimidated into compliance (see more fully, Chapter 3 below).

---

[3] For influential early discussions of punishment as involving censure as an essential feature, see J Feinberg, *Doing and Deserving* (Princeton, Princeton University Press, 1970) Ch 5; R Wasserstrom, *Philosophy and Social Issues: Five Studies.* (Notre Dame, Indiana, University of Notre Dame Press, 1980).

[4] This view of censure's role was developed in A von Hirsch, Past or Future Crimes: Deservedness and Dangerousness in the Sentencing of Criminals (New Brunswick, New Jersey, Rutgers University Press; United Kingdom edn 1986 (Manchester, Manchester University Press, 1985)) Ch 4; von Hirsch 1993, Ch 2; see also U Narayan, 'Adequate Responses and Preventive Benefits: Justifying Censure and Hard Treatment in Legal Punishment' (1993) *Oxford Journal of Legal Studies* 13, 166. For further discussion, see AE Bottoms, 'Five Puzzles in von Hirsch's Theory' in A Ashworth and M Wasik (eds), *Fundamentals of Sentencing Theory: Essays in Honour of Andrew von Hirsch* (Oxford, Oxford University Press, 1998) 77–95, and A von Hirsch and A Ashworth, *Proportionate Sentencing: Exploring the Principles* (Oxford, Oxford University Press, 2005) Ch 2.

Relying on this idea of censure helps remove some of the seeming mysteriousness of penal desert judgments. Censure or blaming involves everyday normative judgments that are used in a wide variety of social contexts, of which punishment is merely one. The account also helps address another objection traditionally raised against retributive penal theories, namely, their seeming harshness—their apparent insistence on an eye for an eye. Once the 'paying back' of evil for evil is no longer viewed as the underlying idea, penal desert does not demand visitation upon the offender of as much suffering as he had inflicted on his victim. What is called for instead is punishments that are *proportionate* to the seriousness of the criminal conduct. Proportionate punishments, even when not involving harm-for-harm equivalence, would suffice to convey disapprobation for various crimes according to their degree of reprehensibility. Indeed, a desert perspective supports substantial *reductions* of existing penalty levels, as will be explained below (Chapter 4).

Punishment conveys disapprobation, but does so in a special way—through visitation of deprivation ('hard treatment') on the offender. The hard treatment is the vehicle through which the censure is expressed. But why use this vehicle, rather than expressing blame in a purely symbolic fashion?

The reason for having the institution of punishment—that is, for expressing disapproval through the infliction of penal deprivation instead of merely censuring—has to do with keeping predatory behaviour within tolerable limits. Had the criminal sanction no usefulness in preventing crime, there might be no need to visit deprivations on those who offend. We might, instead, try to devise other ways of issuing authoritative judgments of disapproval, for such predatory behaviour as occurs. But those judgments, in the interest of keeping state-inflicted deprivation to a minimum, would no longer have to be linked to purposive infliction of penal deprivation (see more fully, Chapter 3).

If the criminal sanction aims to prevent crime as well as censure, how is this consistent with treating offenders and potential offenders as moral agents? The hard treatment in punishment, in my view, serves a prudential reason for obedience to those who would be insufficiently motivated by the penal censure's normative appeal. But this should *supplement* rather than replace the moral reasons for desistance from crime conveyed by the penal censure—that is, it provides an *additional* reason for compliance to those who are deemed capable of recognising the law's moral demands, but who are also tempted to disobey them nevertheless. The criminal law thus addresses *ourselves*, not a distinct 'criminal class' of those considered incapable of grasping moral appeals. And it addresses us neither as perfectly moral agents (we are not angels), nor as beasts that can only be made to comply through threats. Instead, the criminal law addresses us as moral but fallible agents, who may also need prudential inducements to help us resist criminal temptation (see more fully, Chapter 3 below). However, this account (as will be discussed in Chapter 5 below) calls for moderation in the overall severity in punishment levels. The harsher the penalty system is, the less plausible it becomes to see it as embodying a moral appeal rather than a system of bare threats.

2.2 THE RATIONALE FOR PROPORTIONALITY

In a minimal sense, proportionality always had a role in sentencing policy: penalties that are grossly excessive in relation to the gravity of the offence have commonly been understood as being unfair. Statutory maximum sentences reflect that understanding, which also has had a constitutional dimension: various jurisdictions have adopted a constitutional bar against grossly excessive punishments. This, however, gives the notions of desert only an outer constraining role, of barring manifestly harsh sanctions for lesser offences. Short of these (rather high) maximum limits, proportionality long had received scant consideration in sentencing policy, with crime-prevention concerns emphasised instead. What is distinctive about contemporary desert theory is that it moves the notion of proportionality from such a peripheral to a central role in deciding the severity of penalties. The primary basis for deciding quanta of sentences, on the desert model, is the principle of proportionality—requiring the severity of the sanction to be fairly proportionate to the gravity of the defendant's criminal conduct.

The concept of proportionality of which I am speaking is different from the notion of 'proportionality' that is employed in human-rights jurisprudence. The latter idea is prospectively-oriented and concerned with the suitability of means to ends: an intervention is thus deemed 'disproportionate' if it utilises unduly burdensome or intrusive means in order to achieve ends of comparatively little importance.[5]

---

[5] See, eg, I Cameron, *An Introduction to the European Convention on Human Rights*, 3rd edn (Uppsala, Iustus, 1998).

Proportionality in sentencing theory is concerned not with such a prospective means-ends relationship, but operates instead *retrospectively*. It concerns the relationship between the severity of the punishment to be imposed, and the gravity of the offence for which the defendant stands convicted.

What is the basis for this (retrospective) principle of proportionality? The censure account, just discussed, provides the explanation. If punishment embodies blame, then the degree of severity imposed would convey how much the conduct is to be disapproved. If crime *X* is punished more severely than crime *Y*, this connotes the greater disapprobation of crime *X*. Punishments, consequently, should be allocated consistently with their blaming implications. When penalties are arrayed in severity according to the gravity of offences, the degree of disapprobation thereby conveyed would then be consistent with the degree of reprehensibility of the conduct involved. When punishments are arrayed otherwise, this may not merely be inefficient (who knows?—it might sometimes 'work'), but unfair; offenders would be visited with greater or less disapprobation than the degree of blameworthiness that their conduct would warrant (see more fully, Chapter 4).

Fairness is sacrificed when the proportionality principle is disregarded even when this is done for the sake of crime prevention. Suppose that offenders A and B commit and are convicted of criminal conduct of approximately the same degree of seriousness. Suppose, however, that B is deemed more likely to reoffend, and therefore is given a substantially longer prison sentence. Notwithstanding any enhanced crime preventive utility of that sentence, the objection remains that B, through his more severe punishment, is being treated as having behaved more reprehensibly than A, although their conduct actually had the same degree of blameworthiness.

2.3 PROPORTIONALITY AS 'LIMITING' OR 'DETERMINING'?

If the principle of proportionality is so important, is it a 'determining' or merely a 'limiting' principle? While our sense of justice tells us that criminals should be punished consistently with the seriousness of their offences, there do not seem to be definite quanta of severity associated with those desert judgments. Armed robbers have committed a serious offence, deserving of substantial punishment, but it is not immediately apparent whether that should ordinarily consist of three years' confinement, five years, or some shorter or longer period.

A possible response to this problem has been to assert that desert is merely a 'limiting' principle:[6] It tells us, supposedly, not how much robbers deserve, but only provides broad limits beyond which their punishments would be *un*deserved. Within such outer limits, the sentence may then be decided on other grounds—for example, on the basis of the defendant's estimated likelihood of reoffending. This view would mean, however, that persons who commit similar crimes could receive very different amounts of punishment. If punishment embodies blame as a central characteristic, it becomes morally problematic to visit such different degrees of severity (and hence of implicit disapprobation) for comparably blameworthy transgressions. An alternative account, but scarcely a plausible one, would be a heroic intuitionist stance: that if we only were to reflect deeply enough, we should be able to perceive specific deserved quanta of punishments: that robbers deserve so-and-so many years and months of confinement, and so forth. Our intuitions, however, hardly seem so precise.

The way out of this difficulty is to recognise the crucial difference between the comparative ranking of punishments on one hand, and the overall magnitude and anchoring points of the scale of penalties on the other. With respect to comparative rankings, *ordinal* proportionality provides considerable guidance. Persons convicted of crimes of similar seriousness should receive punishments of comparable severity; and persons convicted of crimes of differing seriousness should suffer punishments correspondingly graded in onerousness. These ordinal-proportionality requirements are no mere limits, and would be infringed were equally reprehensible conduct punished unequally (see Chapter 5).

Desert provides less guidance, however, on the overall dimensions and anchoring points of the scale of penalties. This is because the

---

[6] This view has been identified with the writings of Norval Morris; see N Morris, *Punishment, Desert, and Rehabilitation* (Washington DC, US Government Printing Office, 1976); N Morris, *Madness and the Criminal Law* (Chicago, Chicago University Press, 1982) Ch 5. This view also has modern proponents, but with significantly revised arguments, see RS Frase, *Just Sentencing: Principles and Procedures for a Workable System* (New York, Oxford University Press, 2013). For further discussion, see ch 9 below.

censure expressed through penal deprivations is, in part, a convention. When the penalty structure reflects the comparative gravity of crimes, making *pro rata* decreases or increases in the various prescribed sanctions could constitute just a change in that convention.

This distinction helps resolve the dilemma just mentioned. The leeway which desert allows in fixing the penalty system's overall degree of onerousness explains why we cannot perceive a single 'right' or 'fitting' penalty for a crime. Whether *X* months, *Y* months, or somewhere in between is the appropriate penalty for a given type of crime would depend significantly on how the penalty structure has been anchored and what punishments are prescribed for other crimes. Once those anchoring points are decided, however, the more restrictive requirements of ordinal proportionality come to apply. This explains why it would be inappropriate to give short prison terms to some convicted criminals and lengthy prison terms to other criminals convicted of similar criminal conduct, on the basis (say) of predictive factors not reflecting the comparative degree of seriousness of their conduct.

2.4 GAUGING CRIMES' SERIOUSNESS AND PUNISHMENTS' SEVERITY

The rank-ordering requirement of proportionality presupposes a capacity to rank different types of crimes according to their seriousness. How can such judgements of crime-seriousness be accomplished?

The seriousness of crime has two main elements: the conduct's degree of harmfulness (or dangerousness), and the extent of the actor's culpability. With respect to culpability, the substantive criminal law can be of some help—because its theories of fault have analogues for sentencing theory. The substantive criminal law, for example, distinguishes intentional (ie, purposive, knowing or reckless) conduct from negligent conduct.[7] Sentencing theory could make fuller use of such distinctions (although those implications have yet to be spelled out in detail).

---

[7] For such a classification of degrees of intent, see eg American Law Institute, Model Penal Code (1962), s 2.02 (2), see also, A Ashworth, *Sentencing and Criminal Justice*, 6th edn (Cambridge, Cambridge University Press, 2015) 157–59.

With harm, the problem has been to compare the degree of injuriousness of criminal acts that invade differing interests—to compare simple thefts of property with (say) invasions of privacy of the home. Here, a broad notion of quality of life can be helpful: invasions of different interests can be compared according to the extent to which they typically affect a person's *standard of living*—understood in a broad sense of that term, which takes into account non-economic as well as economic wellbeing.[8] Such an analysis facilitates comparisons. Burglary and assault, for example, may affect diverse interests, but they nevertheless may be compared in their impact on a standard person's quality of life. This method of analysis is explained more fully in Chapter 6.

The living-standard idea can also be helpful in comparing the severity of various penalties. Severity can be gauged—not in terms of individual offenders' differing personal sensitivities—but rather in terms of how various sanctions *typically* would affect the interests that characterise the quality of someone's existence (see Chapter 6).

2.5 ROLE OF PREVIOUS CRIMINAL CONVICTIONS

Another issue that desert theorists have addressed is the role of an offender's previous criminal convictions. Most penal systems adjust the severity of the sentence to reflect the defendant's prior criminal history, but it has been a matter of controversy why there should be such an adjustment, and how much weight the person's prior criminal record should have. A predictive rationale for sentencing would give principal emphasis to previous arrests and convictions, as those factors are most strongly predictive of future offending.[9] Desert theory, by contrast,

---

[8] This living-standard analysis of criminal harm was developed in A von Hirsch and N Jareborg, 'Gauging Criminal Harm: A Living-Standard Analysis' (1991) *Oxford Journal of Legal Studies* 11, 1. It draws on the conception of the living-standard conceived by the philosopher and economist Amartya Sen; A Sen, *The Standard of Living* (Cambridge, Cambridge University Press, 1987). See more fully, ch 6 below.

[9] See National Academy of Sciences, Panel on Research on Criminal Careers (1986). 'Criminal Careers and "Career Criminals"' (edited by A Blumstein, J Cohen, J Roth and C Visher) (Washington DC, National Academies of Sciences Press, 1986) Vol 1; von Hirsch 1985, Chs 7, 11.

should give principal weight to the gravity of the current offence; that is, indeed, a salient operational difference between prediction-based and desert-based schemes. But the question remains, whether a desert rationale would permit the criminal record to be given any weight, and if so how much.

Some desert theorists, including myself, have argued for a modest adjustment in sentence on account of the defendant's prior record—in the form of a limited penalty discount for first offenders or for those with modest records of previous convictions.[10] This (as will be argued more fully in Chapter 7 below) can be seen as a way of recognising human fallibility in the criteria for punishment. By giving the first offender a somewhat scaled-down punishment, he is censured for his criminal act but nevertheless accorded some respect for the fact that his inhibitions against wrongdoing appear to have functioned on previous occasions, and some sympathy or tolerance for the all-too-human frailty that can lead to such a lapse. With repetition, however, this extenuation diminishes and eventually is lost. While this approach permits a limited differentiation to be made on the basis of prior convictions, however, the primary emphasis will remain on the gravity of the current offence.

2.6 INCLUSION OF CRIME-CONTROL AIMS?

Desert theory sets priorities among sentencing aims: it assumes that it is more important to have proportionately-ordered sanctions than to seek other objectives such as restraining offenders who are deemed higher risks. This understandably evokes discomfort: why cannot one seek proportionality *and* pursue other desired ends, whether they be treatment, incapacitation or deterrence?

To some extent, desert theory permits consideration of other aims: namely, to the degree that this is consistent with the proportionate ordering of penalties. Thus, when there is a choice between two non-custodial sanctions of approximately equivalent severity, proportionality

---

[10] See Ashworth 2015, Ch 6; A von Hirsch, 'Proportionality and the Progressive Loss of Mitigation: Some Further Reflections' in A von Hirsch and JV Roberts (eds), *Previous Convictions at Sentencing: Theoretical and Applied Perspectives* (Oxford, Hart Publishing, 2010) Ch 1.

constraints are not offended when one of these sanctions is chosen over the other on (say) rehabilitative grounds. Desert theorists thus have come forward with schemes for utilising intermediate, non-custodial penalties. These penalties would be ranked in severity according to the gravity of the crime, but penalties of roughly equivalent onerousness could be substituted for one another when (say) treatment concerns so indicate (see Chapter 8). Nevertheless, a desert model has this important constraint: that such ulterior aims could be relied upon only when this would not substantially disturb the proportionate ranking of penalties. Giving substantial extra prison time to persons deemed to constitute higher risks of reoffending would thus breach the model's requirements. Why not, then, relax the model's constraints to allow more scope to such other aspirations?

A possibility—sometimes referred to as a 'modified' desert model—would be to relax the desert constraints to a limited extent. Proportionality would primarily determine comparative punishment levels, but modest deviations from the deserved sentence would be deemed permissible. While such departures involve a sacrifice of equity, the extent of that sacrifice would depend on the degree of the deviation from desert constraints. Limited deviations, arguably, could permit the pursuit of ulterior objectives without 'too much' unfairness (see more fully, Chapter 9).

These mixed approaches would still make desert the primary determinant for the ordering of penalties, but grant some extra scope for other purposes. Such schemes remain significantly constraining, however. Some extra leeway might be given, say, to suit a non-custodial penalty to the offender's apparent treatment needs, but not a great deal.

Could still more scope be given to non-desert considerations? With a mixed rationale, either desert will predominate or some other aim will. If—in the ordinary case—the seriousness of the crime is the penalty's primary determinant, the system remains desert-dominated. However, if other (say, crime-preventive) aims are given primary emphasis, that creates a system dominated by those aims. That will reintroduce the familiar problems of consequentialist sentencing schemes—for example, those relating to inequitable outcomes, and to insufficient systematic knowledge of preventive effects (see Chapter 1 above).

In assessing these alternatives, it needs to be borne in mind that even a 'purely' desert-based sentencing scale is likely to have collateral crime-prevention benefits—in such deterrence as its penalties can achieve, and in the incapacitative effects of the prison sentences it imposes for more serious crimes. Departing from proportionality for the sake of crime prevention, then, should not just call for a showing that some preventative effect might be achieved (for a desert-based system might also have such collateral effects). Instead, it would call for a showing that the departures from proportionality are likely to yield significantly *greater* preventative effects—which will be no easy matter to establish. And here, one is likely to confront a fairness/effectiveness trade-off: because crime rates tend to be insensitive to small variations in punishment, limited departures from proportionality may have scant crime-preventive impact; large departures might possibly prevent crime better, but these precisely are the ones that are most troublesome on fairness grounds.

2.7 DESERT AND INCREASED PENAL SEVERITY?

Does the desert model lead to harsher penalties? As that model emerged and became influential at a time when penalty levels rose in many jurisdictions, some critics have argued that the theory must be responsible for such increases. However, desert itself does not call for harsher penalties—indeed, as noted already, it permits (indeed, points toward) considerable penalty reductions.[11] Moreover, the sentence-reform schemes which rely explicitly on notions of desert have tended to utilise more moderate sanctions: the Minnesota sentencing guidelines, for example, call for penalties that have been well below prevailing US norms. European proportionality-oriented sentencing standards, such as those of Finland and Sweden, are likewise associated with penal moderation. Measures which most clearly call for tougher sanctions tend to utilise criteria inconsistent with proportionality: mandatory minimum sentences, for example, select particular offence categories for harsh treatment, without regard to the gravity of the offence involved, or the penalties imposed for other kinds of offences.

---

[11] See more fully ch 10 below.

3

Why Should the Criminal Sanction Exist?

3.1 VARIETIES OF DESERT THEORIES

DESERT, IN ORDINARY parlance, refers to certain kinds of reasons for a favourable or an unfavourable response to someone's behaviour. Those reasons are ones concerning the good or bad qualities of the person's conduct. A person may be said to deserve something positive in virtue of his fine work or generous acts; or something undesirable in virtue of his reprehensible behaviour. The concept is not directed to the future: by saying that A deserves X, one is not saying that he, or someone else, or society in general will necessarily be better off if he gets X. Rather, the concept is retrospectively oriented. One is saying that X is A's due because of the quality of what he *has* done.[1]

A desert-based penal theory, in the broadest sense, is one that rests the decision to punish, in part or entirely, on claims that the convicted offender deserves it. But why should punishment be deserved? A variety of explanations exist.[2]

A traditional retributive account has been that of requital-for-evil. The doing of a wrong, according to this view, generates a moral obligation to inflict reciprocal suffering on the wrongdoer: the wrongdoer should be 'paid back' or 'requited' for his wrong.[3] The theory is open to serious objection. First, it is seldom made clear *why* such requital is required. Some defenders of the view assert this is a matter of

[1] See also, A von Hirsch and A Ashworth, *Proportionate Sentencing: Exploring the Principles* (Oxford, Oxford University Press, 2005) Ch 2.

[2] For an overview of various retributive theories, see J Ryberg, *The Ethics of Proportionate Punishment: A Critical Investigation* (Dordrecht, Kluwer Academic Publishers, 2007).

[3] For a recent statement of this view, see RL Lippke, *Rethinking Imprisonment* (New York, Oxford University Press, 2007).

elementary moral intuition,[4] but this scarcely constitutes a helpful explanation. Second, a requital theory, insofar as it provides any guidance at all, would seem to point to harm-for-harm equivalence: the offender should be made to suffer as much as he hurt the victim. In short, the theory would call for something akin to a *lex talionis*, rather than a requirement of proportionate sanctions.

Another more recent perspective is the 'unfair advantage theory'.[5] This account focusses on the criminal law as a jointly beneficial enterprise. The law requires each person to desist from specified kinds of misconduct. By so desisting, the person benefits others; but he himself also benefits from their reciprocal self-restraint. The person who victimises others while benefiting from their self-restraint thus obtains an unjust advantage. Punishment's supposed role is to impose an offsetting disadvantage.

The theory has various perplexities. It might be argued that the offender, by benefitting from others' self-restraint, has a reciprocal obligation to restrain himself. It is far more obscure, however, to assert that if he disregards that obligation and does offend, the 'advantage' (of extra freedom of action) that he supposedly gains might somehow be eliminated or cancelled (in other than a purely metaphorical sense) by punishing him.[6] The theory would also distort the way in which offenders' penal deserts are assessed. There is much artificiality in assessing how much punishment is deserved for typical victimising

---

[4] The American penal theorist Michael Moore takes such a view; see M Moore, *Placing Blame: A General Theory of Criminal Law* (Oxford, Clarendon Press, 1997) Chs 3 and 4.

[5] For a recent discussion of the 'unfair advantage' theory, see J Staihar, 'Proportionality and Punishment' (2015) *Iowa Law Review* 100, 1209–32; for earlier accounts, see J Finnis, *Natural Law and Natural Rights* (Oxford, Oxford University Press, 1980); M Davis, Michael (1983), 'How to Make the Punishment Fit the Crime' (1983) *Ethics* 93, 726. In my book *Doing Justice*, I partially endorsed this theory, but shortly thereafter developed doubts, and argued against it in subsequent volumes; compare A von Hirsch, *Doing Justice: The Choice of Punishments* (New York, Hill and Wang, 1976); Reprinted 1986 (Boston: Northeastern University Press)) Ch 6 with A von Hirsch, *Past or Future Crimes: Deservedness and Dangerousness in the Sentencing of Criminals* (New Brunswick, New Jersey, Rutgers University Press, 1985); United Kingdom edn 1986 (Manchester, Manchester University Press)) 57–59 and 7–8.

[6] See A von Hirsch, *Censure and Sanctions* (Oxford, Oxford University Press, 1993) 7–8; and RA Duff, *Trials and Punishments* (Cambridge, Cambridge University Press, 1986) Ch 9.

crimes, such as armed robbery, in terms of the extra freedom-of-action that the robber supposedly gains over uninvolved third parties, rather than in terms of the blameworthiness of the conduct's intrusion into the legitimate interests of victims.

3.2 CENSURE-BASED JUSTIFICATIONS FOR PUNISHMENT

Censure-based accounts of the institution of the criminal sanction are those that focus on the institution's blaming features. The penal sanction manifestly does convey blame. Punishing someone consists of visiting a deprivation ('hard treatment') on him, because he has committed a wrong, in a manner that expresses disapprobation of the person for his misdeed. Treating the offender as a wrongdoer, the American moral philosopher Richard Wasserstrom has pointed out,[7] is central to the idea of punishment. The difference between a tax and a fine does not rest in the kind of material deprivation involved (money in both cases). It consists, rather, in the fact that the fine conveys disapprobation or censure, whereas tax ordinarily does not.[8]

An account of the criminal sanction which emphasises this reprobative function has the attraction of being comprehensible, because blaming is something we do in everyday moral judgements. A censure-based account is also linked more clearly to proportionality. If punishment involves the ascription of blame, then it seems to follow that the ordering of penalties for different crimes should reflect the degree of blameworthiness of those offences.

A desert-based theory of legal punishment must thus assume that criminal conduct is, in some sense, wrongful. Censure-based theories clearly have this presupposition, for the conduct is treated as warranting disapprobation. Criminal prohibitions of today have wide scope, however, and include some kinds of conduct that seem in no obvious way reprehensible. A censure-based theory of punishment, however,

---

[7] R Wasserstrom, *Philosophy and Social Issues: Five Studies* (Notre Dame, Indiana, University of Notre Dame Press, 1980); see also, J Feinberg, *Doing and Deserving* (Princeton, Princeton University Press, 1970) Ch 5.

[8] For a discussion of the hard treatment concept in punishment, see also J Kleinig, John (2011). 'What Does Wrongdoing Deserve?' in M Tonry (ed), *Retributivism Has a Past. Has It a Future?* (New York, Oxford University Press, 2011) Ch 3.

need not defend all such prohibitions. It suffices if the core conduct with which the criminal law deals can legitimately be characterised as blameworthy, because it does harm to its victims (eg, violence or theft), creates unwarranted risks of injury (eg, drinking and driving), or involves the flouting of important communal obligations (eg, tax evasion). Indeed, treating the criminal law as essentially involving censure provides a 'critical edge': it provides reason for decriminalising conduct that cannot reasonably be accounted for as being wrongful in some fashion.[9]

A censure-based account, of the sort of which I am speaking here, treats the blame in punishment as a response that may be justifiably directed to the criminal actor, seen as a person capable of moral deliberation. Certain conduct is deemed reprehensible, and the blaming response is supposed to convey the degree of disapprobation that is fairly warranted for the conduct.

The censuring response must be one that can be explained to the person who is being blamed, assuming that he is capable of understanding normative reasons for action or desistance. Censure, in this sense, is different from mere *denunciation*.[10] Denunciatory theories treat the punished offender solely as a conduit for messages of public abhorrence of crime and of criminals—and thus may be wholly lacking in fairness requirements. An American penal theorist, taking such a view, has indeed argued in favour of humiliating punishments—in which proportionality requirements would be largely or wholly absent.[11]

3.3 WHY THE CENSURE IN PUNISHMENT?

That punishment conveys blame or disapprobation is evident enough. But why *should* there be a blaming response to the conduct with which the criminal law deals? Without an answer to that question, legal punishment might possibly be replaced by an alternative kind of response

---

[9] See more fully, AP Simester and A von Hirsch, *Crimes, Harms, and Wrongs. On the Principles of Criminalisation* (Oxford, Hart Publishing, 2011) Chs 1 and 2.

[10] On denunciation in punishment, see N Walker, *Why Punish?* (Oxford, Oxford University Press, 1991).

[11] DM Kahan, 'What Do Alternative Sanctions Mean?' (1996) *University of Chicago Law Review* 63, 591.

that has no censuring implications—for example something akin to a tax, meant to discourage specified behaviour.

PF Strawson, the late Oxford philosopher, provides a starting point.[12] Responding to wrongdoing by reprobation or censure, he asserts, is simply part of a morality that holds people accountable for their conduct. When a person commits a misdeed, others judge him adversely, because his conduct was reprehensible. Censure consists of the expression of that judgement, plus its accompanying sentiment of disapproval. One would withhold this expression of blame only if there were special reasons for not confronting the actor: for example, doubts about his mental capacity, or about one's own standing to challenge him for what he has done.

Strawson's account is helpful because blaming *does* seem part of a morality holding people accountable for their actions. However, it is worth specifying some further features of blaming. First, censure considers the victim. He or she has not only been injured, but *wronged* through someone's culpable act. It thus would not suffice just to acknowledge that the injury has occurred or to convey sympathy to victims (as when people have been injured through a natural disaster). Censure, by directing disapprobation at the person responsible, acknowledges that the victim's hurt occurred through that person's fault.[13]

Second and more importantly, censure addresses the act's perpetrator. He is conveyed a critical message concerning the impropriety of his conduct, namely that he culpably has mistreated someone, and is being visited with disapprobation for having done so. Some moral response on his part would ordinarily be assumed to be appropriate—for example, an expression of concern, an effort at better self-restraint; or else, a plea in justification or excuse for the conduct.[14]

---

[12] P Strawson, *Freedom and Resentment and Other Essays* (London, Methuen, 1974) Ch 1.

[13] See more fully von Hirsch 1993, Ch 2; A von Hirsch and A Ashworth, *Proportionate Sentencing: Exploring the Principles* (Oxford, Oxford University Press, 2005) Ch 2. Compared to everyday contexts, the criminal law restricts more narrowly the grounds for such justifications and excuses. But even non-criminal contexts will have some such restrictions; consider, for example, what kind of excuses would and would not be deemed acceptable in an academic disciplinary proceeding.

[14] Ibid.

The disapproval conveyed by the sanction gives the actor the opportunity to reconsider his actions and to feel shame or regret. However, it should be up to him whether so to respond. I am not putting forward a penance theory, according to which the punitive response would specially be fashioned to elicit certain sentiments in him, such as shame or repentance.[15] There thus should be no need, in my view, to tailor the censuring response to the actor's supposed degree of receptiveness. Fashioning a sanction so as to induce repentant attitudes might be an appropriate mission for an abbot dealing with the sins of an erring novice, but it scarcely seems an appropriate role for a modern state.[16]

The criminal law gives the censure it expresses yet another important role: that of addressing third parties (namely, members of the public) and providing them with reason for desistance. Unlike blame in everyday contexts, the criminal sanction announces in advance that specified categories of conduct are punishable. Because the prescribed sanction is one which expresses disapprobation, this conveys publicly the message that the conduct is deemed reprehensible, and should be thus eschewed. It is not necessarily a matter of teaching that the conduct is wrong, for those addressed (or many of them) may well understand that already. Rather, the censure embodied in the prescribed sanction serves to *appeal* to people's sense of the conduct's wrongfulness, as a reason for desistance.

However, the normative message expressed in penal statutes is not reducible (as Scandinavian and German advocates of *positive general prevention* have contended)[17] to an inducement to law-abidingness that is utilised because the citizenry may be more responsive to moral appeals than to bare threats. In my view, the censure expressed through punishment is legitimated through its being an ethically appropriate way of

---

[15] Ibid. Such a penance theory has been put forward by the British penal theorist RA Duff.

[16] See RA Duff, *Punishment, Communication, and Community* (New York, Oxford University Press, 2001), accompanying text to nn 33–34.

[17] J Andenaes, *Punishment and Deterrence* (Ann Arbor, Michigan, University of Michigan Press, 1982); for an extended critical discussion of positive general prevention, see the essays collected in B Schünemann, A von Hirsch and N Jareborg, *Positive Generalprävention: Kritische Perspektiven in deutsch-englischem Dialog* (Heidelberg, CF Müller, 1998).

addressing the perpetrator and third persons, seen as agents capable of moral deliberation. The collateral crime-preventative effect that such messages may have is secondary to such normative claims. Censuring a person cannot morally be justified, however, *merely* in terms of its possible effects in inducing other persons (or the actor himself) to develop better internalised commitments to law-abidingness.[18]

The foregoing account of censure's role explains why the misconduct should not be dealt solely through neutral sanctions that convey no disapproval. Exclusive reliance on such sanctions—even if they were no less effective in discouraging the behaviour—would disregard the person's status as an agent capable of moral understanding. A system solely of neutral sanctions would treat offenders or potential offenders much as beasts in a circus, that need to be restrained or intimidated into desistance from injurious behaviour because they are deemed incapable of understanding why injuring people is wrong. Condemnatory sanctions treat the actor as a *person* who is capable of such understanding.

A committed utilitarian might insist that treating the actor as a person in this fashion could only be warranted on instrumental grounds.[19] This, however, is reductionist. Addressing the actor as someone capable of moral choice, rather than as a creature to be intimidated or controlled, is a matter of acknowledging his status as a responsible agent. Is this acknowledgement warranted only if it leads to beneficial social consequences? Those consequences would not necessarily have to be those of crime prevention—for it might be possible to devise a 'neutral' sanction (one designed to impose material deprivation but convey no blame) that could also help prevent crime. Or might society have better cohesion if actors are treated as being responsible, and hence subject to censure for their actions? Making such arguments would involve trying to reduce ethical judgements to difficult-to-confirm empirical surmises. While one can have some confidence in the ethical judgement that offenders should be treated as agents capable of choice, it would be much more difficult to determine whether so treating them will necessarily lead to a more smoothly-running society.

---

[18] See more fully, von Hirsch and Ashworth 2005, 133–34.
[19] See, Walker 1991.

3.4 WHY THE HARD TREATMENT IN PUNISHMENT?

Punishment involves censure, but it does not consist *only* in censure. The censure is expressed through *hard treatment*:[20] that is, through a deprivation that is visited on the convicted offender. It is thus necessary to address punishment's other constitutive element: the deprivation or 'hard treatment'.

A desert theorist, John Kleinig,[21] has asserted that notions of censure can also account for the hard treatment feature in punishment. He argues that censure (at least in certain social contexts) cannot be expressed adequately in purely verbal or symbolic terms; that hard treatment is needed to show that the disapproval is meant seriously. For example, an academic department would not show its disapprobation of a serious lapse by a colleague through a mere verbal admonition; to convey the requisite disapprobation, a curtailment of privileges would be called for. This justification has plausibility outside legal contexts, where the deprivations involved are modest enough to serve chiefly to underline the intended disapproval. However, I do not think that the argument suffices to account for the criminal sanction.

The criminal law has preventive features in its very design. When the state criminalises conduct, it issues a legal threat: that such conduct is proscribed, and violation will result in the imposition of specified sanctions. The threat appears to be aimed explicitly at discouraging the proscribed conduct.[22] Criminal sanctions also appear to be too onerous to serve merely to give credibility to the censure. Even if penalties were substantially scaled down, some of them still could involve significant deprivations of liberty or property. In the absence of a preventive purpose, it is hard to conceive of such onerous intrusions as having the sole function of showing that the expression of disapproval is seriously intended.

---

[20] The term 'hard treatment' was coined by the American legal philosopher Joel Feinberg to denote the deprivation element in punishment; Feinberg 1970, Ch 5. For further discussion, see M Matravers, 'Is Twenty-first Century Punishment Post-Desert?' in M Tonry (ed), *Retributivism Has a Past: Has It a Future?* (New York, Oxford University Press, 2011) Ch 2.

[21] J Kleinig, 'Punishment and Moral Seriousness' (1991) *Israel Law Review* 25, 401.

[22] See more fully, Simester and von Hirsch 2011, Ch 1.

The crime-preventative features of the criminal law are vitally important, moreover, because criminal behaviour is profoundly threatening to citizens' vital interests: to their physical safety and to their living resources. It is thus essential that the criminal sanction should serve to help discourage such behaviour.[23]

The foregoing arguments led me to suggest, in a 1985 volume,[24] a bifurcated account of punishment. The criminal law, I asserted, performs two interlocking functions. By threatening unpleasant consequences, it seeks to discourage criminal behaviour. Through the censure thereby expressed, the sanction also registers disapprobation of the behaviour. Citizens are thus provided with normative as well as prudential reasons for compliance.

However, the two elements, reprobation and prevention, seemed in my 1985 account to be uneasily matched. Whereas the censuring element appeals to the person's moral agency, would not the preventive element play merely upon his fear of unpleasant consequences? If the person is capable of being moved by moral appeals, why the threat? If not capable and thus in need of the threat, is he not being treated like a dangerous beast? A clarification of the preventive function—and its relation to the censuring function—was needed.

I attempted such a clarification in a subsequent (1993) volume.[25] The preventive function of the sanction, I argued, supplies a prudential reason that is tied to, and supplements, the normative reason conveyed by penal censure. The criminal law, through the disapprobation it embodies, conveys that the conduct is wrong, and a moral agent thus is given grounds for desistance. However, he may (considering human fallibility) be tempted nevertheless. A reason why, in punishment, hard treatment is used as the vehicle for expressing censure (instead of purely symbolic censure being utilised) is that this provides him with a further reason—a prudential one—for resisting the temptation. Indeed, an agent who has accepted the sanction's message that he ought not offend, and who recognises his own susceptibility to temptation, might well favour the existence of a censuring response that embodies such

---

[23] See more fully, A von Hirsch, 'Harm and Wrongdoing in Criminalisation Theory' (2014) *Criminal Law & Philosophy* 8, 245.

[24] von Hirsch 1985, Ch 5.

[25] von Hirsch 1993, Ch 2; For a fuller account of this revised view, see von Hirsch and Ashworth 2005, Ch 2.

a prudential disincentive, as an aid to carrying out what he himself recognises as the proper course of conduct.

A certain conception of human nature, and of reasons for action, underlie this account. Persons, it is assumed, are neither like angels for whom purely normative appeals would suffice, nor like brutes which can be influenced only by threats. Instead, human beings are moral but fallible creatures—capable of being motivated by moral appeals, but tempted to offend nevertheless. A person's character as moral agent makes them capable of taking into consideration the censuring message conveyed through the sanction, that the conduct is reprehensible. Given human fallibility, however, the temptation to offend becomes easier to resist if a disincentive against the conduct is also provided. Providing such a disincentive does not render the sanction purely coercive: it does not make fear of unpleasant consequences the only basis for compliance. It is possible, given this bifurcated account of human nature, to have a response that supplies both moral and prudential reasons for desistance.[26]

An advantage of a censure-based penal theory, I suggested earlier in this chapter, is that it treats the offender as a moral agent: the censure appeals to the agent's capacity for evaluating the appropriateness of his actions. But the rationale I have just suggested is in part preventive, relying on a disincentive against conduct. Does the limited introduction of any such element of crime prevention, even within a censuring framework, vitiate the legitimacy of the response as an appeal to the actor's moral agency?

That depends on how stringently one conceives of moral agency. On a narrow view (sometimes erroneously attributed to Kant)[27] someone is treated as a moral agent only if the reasons for action he is offered are *purely* moral reasons. Introduction of any prudential considerations would divest the appeal of its essential normative character. Such a

---

[26] For further analysis of this issue, see von Hirsch and Ashworth 2005, Ch 2; and also AE Bottoms, 'Five Puzzles in von Hirsch's Theory' in A Ashworth and M Wasik (eds), *Fundamentals of Sentencing Theory: Essays in Honour of Andrew von Hirsch* (Oxford, Oxford University Press, 1998) Ch 3.

[27] Kant's views are actually more differentiated, for he distinguishes between actions having personal moral worth, and reasons which the law may legitimately invoke in its public standards.

perspective, however, scarcely appears to be helpful when considering how a state might properly deal with the actual, fallible human beings that constitute its citizenry.

An alternative, more modest view of moral agency is relied upon in the foregoing account of the role of the hard treatment in punishment. A demand by the state treats the person as a moral agent, in this view, if it offers the actor normative reasons for acting, even if these are not the exclusive reasons. A purely deterrent scheme would not meet this standard: the actor is being informed that he had better comply or else suffer the consequences, but he is being offered no normative reason why he *ought* to comply. On my suggested account, however, the actor *is* given such a normative reason: through the censure embodied in the sanction, the actor is conveyed the message, issued by an authoritative source, that the conduct is reprehensible and thus should be eschewed. Concededly, this is not the *only* reason he is being provided: the censuring response is expressed through hard treatment that serves also to provide a disincentive. But if one accepts the conception of humans that has been propounded here—as fallible agents capable of acting on moral reasons but needing further assistance to withstand such temptation—this still takes the capacity for moral agency seriously.

Notice that I am speaking here of why prevention is in principle a legitimate supporting reason for punishment's existence. I am not speaking of sanctions' overall severity levels, where coerciveness could still become a problem. If overall penalty levels rise sufficiently high, the normative reasons for desistance supplied by penal censure could become overshadowed by the magnitude of the deterrent threat, and thus become of marginal practical significance. If minimal prudence would compel compliance, what difference could the sanction's normative message make? This militates, as I shall elaborate on below (Chapter 5), in favour of keeping the system's overall degree of punitiveness at moderate levels.

3.5 THE RELATION BETWEEN THE TWO ELEMENTS

What is the relation between the two elements in punishment, the reprobative and preventive? We need to be careful that the latter does not operate independently, or else we may undermine the proportionality requirement.

Prevention, on the account of it that I have just given, cannot stand alone, separately from the censuring element. If the sanction conveys censure, it may take a form that also serves as a prudential disincentive, a means for overcoming temptation. But if it *merely* imposes hard treatment, it remains purely coercive. Granted, a morally committed person might find that even a neutral, non-condemnatory sanction makes it easier for him to resist temptation to offend and thus comply with a moral obligation he himself recognises. The sanction would not be respectful of his moral agency, however, if it were couched as a naked threat. Whatever the actor's reasons for compliance, the sanctioning body would be treating him as akin to a beast that needs to be controlled, not as a person for whom normative reasons for acting would matter.

Thus, the structure of my proposed justification for the penal sanction is one in which the blaming function retains a crucial role. A censuring response to injurious conduct, according to this thesis, might possibly be expressed either in a purely symbolic mode; or else, in one in which the reprobation is expressed through the visitation of hard treatment. The criminal sanction is a response of the latter kind. It is preferred to a purely symbolic response because of its supplementary role as a disincentive against criminal behaviour. The preventive function thus operates only *within* a censuring framework.[28]

The censure and the hard treatment are intertwined in the way punishment is structured. A penal measure provides that a specified type of conduct is punishable by certain onerous consequences. Those consequences both constitute the hard treatment and give concrete expression to the censure.[29] Altering those consequences—by raising or lowering the punishment of the conduct within the scale of penalties—will alter the degree of censure conveyed for the behaviour. This intertwining of punishment's blaming and hardtreatment features is crucial for the rationale for proportionality, as we will see in the next chapter.

---

[28] von Hirsch and Ashworth 2005, Ch 2.

[29] Were the hard treatment separable—say, were it assumed that only the conviction expressed censure, and the subsequent penal deprivation had purely preventive functions—then my present account would no longer be sustainable. The deprivation, having no censuring and only a preventive function, would then constitute a bare threat that would no longer address the person as an agent.

My proposed justification of the institution of punishment thus contains both a desert-oriented element concerning censure, and a preventatively-oriented element of providing a disincentive against harmful behaviour. As such it departs from traditional assumptions of European (especially German) penological theory, that the justification for punishment must either be 'relative' (that is, concerned only with crime prevention) or else 'absolute' (that is, based solely on deontological claims of an abstract and universal character). This dichotomy, in my view, seriously interferes with providing a workable account of why the criminal sanction should exist.[30] If punishment is supported purely on crime preventative grounds, then it becomes difficult to justify normative constraints on how much persons may justly be punished. If, on the other hand, it is supported by deontologist appeals to 'absolutes', the explanations tend to be speculative and obscure; and one is also left with the strange conclusion—mentioned by Kant in his famous example of punishment on the island[31]—that it would be necessary to preserve a system of punishing wrongdoers even if no preventative benefits could result from such a practice.

Legal punishment is an institution of the state, and requires as an element of its justification an explanation of the state's involvement. An important deficiency of traditional retributive theories of punishment has been their failure to deal with the state's role in punishing. The foregoing line of argument, I think, helps remedy this deficiency.

---

[30] For a leading German criminal law scholar's recent doubts about this dichotomy, see C Roxin, 'Prevention, Censure and Responsibility: The Recent Debate on the Purposes of Punishment' in AP Simester, A Du Bois-Pedain and U Neumann (eds), *Liberal Criminal Theory: Essays for Andreas von Hirsch* (Oxford, Hart Publishing, 2014) Ch 2, 23–24.

[31] See Kant's example of a hypothetical country located on an island, all of whose members are departing—so that prevention of future criminality would no longer be an issue. If a serious crime were committed just before the inhabitants' departure, should the offender nevertheless be punished—on purely retributive grounds? Kant's example is actually more complicated than it looks, because there is also an issue of consistency: if offenders who committed crimes at an earlier time were punished, why should this last offender be exempt? The consistency problem can be eliminated, however, by altering the hypothetical somewhat. Imagine an island with an unusually peaceable population, in which crimes would be extremely rare even without legal punishment. With the need for prevention largely obviated, must a penal system nevertheless be instituted to punish the rare individuals who do offend? Elsewhere I argue not necessarily—see more fully, this chapter, below.

It is axiomatic that the state has, as one of its major functions that of protecting citizens from harm to their vital interests. It is that mission which warrants the state's prohibition of the kinds of injurious conduct that make up the criminal law. But it is also a duty of the state, I assume, to carry out this function in a manner that treats citizens with respect. A blaming sanction treats those directly affected with respect in a manner that a purely 'neutral' sanction would not, for reasons elaborated on earlier in this chapter.[32]

My two-pronged justification, however, would permit the abolition of the institution of punishment were it not needed for preventive purposes. Imagine a hypothetical society in which social and economic conditions had improved so much that predatory conduct became extremely rare. The criminal sanction—with its armamentarium of courts, correctional agencies, and sanctions—would no longer be required in order to keep such conduct within tolerable levels. Would such a society still be obliged to preserve this institution to deal with the occasional predatory act that might occur? Perhaps not. Such a society might wish to maintain some form of official censure to convey the requisite disapproval of such acts, but with the need for crime prevention largely eliminated, there may no longer be the need for so ambitious, intrusive, and burdensome an institution as the criminal sanction.

During the past three decades, there has existed an alternative retributive conception for punishment: Antony Duff's.[33] There are significant similarities between Duff's model and the desert model described in these pages. Duff's view calls for proportionate sentences, based in substantial part on punishment's censuring implications. His version of proportionality requirements is somewhat more permissive, however, allowing for some additional variation in punishment of comparably serious acts of lawbreaking. His view has attracted extensive academic interest; it has also been influential in penal policy, especially regarding juvenile justice and restorative justice.

Despite their similarities, there is a major difference between Duff's conception and the desert model I describe herein: in their respective accounts of the rationale for punishment's existence. Whereas my account relies on the censuring and crime-preventive features of the

---

[32] See also, von Hirsch 2014.
[33] Duff 1986; Duff 2001.

institution of the criminal sanction (see this chapter), Duff's account emphasises punishment's role as a penance—as providing the offender with a framework for expiating his crime. In our 2005 volume on sentencing theory, Andrew Ashworth and I explain our reservations about his view.[34] Basically, we doubt the state's proper standing to delve so deeply into sentenced offenders' moral attitudes. Such divergences of view may usefully be debated further. But the present volume is not the place, as it aims chiefly at elucidating my version of desert model and its supporting reasons.

For further reading:

Husak, Douglas (2011) 'Why Punish the Deserving?' in D Husak (ed), *Philosophy of Criminal Law: Selected Essays* (Oxford, Oxford University Press) Ch 4.

Kleinig, John (2011) 'What Does Wrongdoing Deserve?' in M Tonry (ed), *Retributivism Has a Past. Has It a Future?* (New York, Oxford University Press) Ch 3.

Matravers, Matt (2011) 'Is Twenty-first Century Punishment Post-Desert?' in Tonry, ibid, Ch 2.

Robinson, Paul H (2001) 'Punishing Dangerousness: Cloaking Preventive Detention as Criminal Justice' *Harvard Law Review* 114, 1429.

Wood, David (2002) 'Retribution, Crime Reduction and the Justification of Punishment. *Oxford Journal of Legal Studies* 22, 301.

---

[34] von Hirsch and Ashworth 2005, Ch 7.

4

Why Punish Proportionately?

I N A MINIMAL sense, proportionality always had a role in
sentencing policy: penalties that were grossly excessive in relation to
the gravity of the offence were perceived as undeserved and unfair.
Statutory maximum penalties reflected that understanding, which also
had a constitutional dimension: several jurisdictions have adopted a
constitutional bar against grossly excessive punishments.[1] Such measures, however, tended to assign proportionality of sentence only a
peripheral role—for example, of barring lengthy prison sentences for
lesser offences.

What is distinctive about contemporary desert theory is that it moves
the idea of proportionality from this peripheral to a central role in
determining sanctions. The primary basis for scaling punishments, the
theory holds, should be the principle of proportionality—requiring the
severity of the penalty to be fairly commensurate with the gravity of
the criminal conduct of which the defendant has been convicted.

It is worth reviewing the justification for this principle. Why should
penalties be proportionate? A variety of possible justifications have
been suggested, some based on crime prevention, and others based
instead on fairness grounds related to the censuring features of punishment. In my view, only the latter can provide a firm basis for the
principle of proportionality.

---

[1] The German Constitutional Court has adopted such a doctrine, barring
grossly disproportionate sanctions; see BVerfGE 50, 125, 133. The US Supreme
Court formerly held that grossly excessive punishments violated the Constitutional
ban on cruel and unusual punishments (see *Weems v US*, 217 US 349 [1911]), but
the Court since has much diluted that doctrine; see Y Lee, 'The Constitutional
Right against Excessive Punishment' (2005) *Virginia Law Review* 91, 677; RS Frase,
'Excessive Prison Sentences, Punishment Goals, and the Eighth Amendment:
Proportionality Relative to What?' (2005) *Minnesota La Review* 89, 571.

4.1 BECCARIA AND BENTHAM'S DETERRENCE ARGUMENT

The first modern defence of the principle of proportionate sanctions was utilitarian, and was formulated two-and-a-half centuries ago by Cesare Beccaria and Jeremy Bentham.[2] These authors advocated a tariff of graded penalties, based on objectives of crime prevention, especially general deterrence. When people offend, they argued, it is preferable that they commit lesser offences rather than serious crimes. Hence, the state should grade its prescribed sanctions according to the seriousness of the offence, so that potential offenders would be induced (should they be inclined to offend at all) to opt for petty thefts instead of burglaries, and burglaries instead of violent crimes. Failure to observe the principle of proportionality in punishing would result in a misdirected structure of disincentives. Persons choosing to offend would thus as soon commit grave crimes as lesser ones.[3]

This account, however, would leave the proportionality principle weak and exception-prone. To avoid sentencing policies' creating perverse incentives, it would be advisable to have penalties scaled ordinarily in some approximate relationship to the gravity of crimes. But there might, under this approach, be substantial exceptions—for example, the imposition of exemplary punishments upon selected intermediate-level crimes, in order to deter these crimes more effectively. When

---

[2] See J Bentham, *An Introduction to the Principles of Morals and Legislation* (JH Byrne and HLA Hart (eds)) (London, Methuen, 1982 (Original 1789)) 168; C Beccaria, *Of Crimes and Punishments* (translated by Henry Paolucci) (Indianapolis, Bobbs-Merrill, 1963 (Original 1764)). For modern variations of these eighteenth century penologists' arguments, see G Stigler, 'The Optimum Enforcement of Laws' (1970) *Journal of Political Economy* 78, 526; DW Friedman and W Sjöström (1993), 'Hanged for a Sheep—the Economics of Marginal Deterrence' (1993) *Journal of Legal Studies* 22, 345.

[3] A problem with this argument is our limited knowledge regarding deterrent effects. To decide sentencing policy on the basis of deterrence, one would need to be able to gauge how much the rates of various crimes are affected by changes in penalties. We are still far from having reliable information of this sort—and such evidence as exists suggests that crime rates are not much influenced by changes in sentence severity levels (see AE Bottoms and A von Hirsch, 'The Crime-Preventive Impact of Penal Sanctions' in P Cane and HM Kritzer (eds), *The Oxford Handbook of Empirical Legal Studies* (Oxford, Oxford University Press, 2010) Ch 4, 98–106). Thus there is little evidence to support the claim that were proportionality not observed, offenders would tend to commit more numerous serious crimes.

the proportionality principle is thus defended on grounds of crime-preventive efficacy and nothing more, then it loses its status as an independent ethical requirement and can be subject to whatever dilutions appear to be needed in the name of crime prevention.

4.2 POSITIVE GENERAL PREVENTION: THE INHIBITION-REINFORCEMENT ARGUMENT

European penologists, even when utilitarian in general outlook, have tended to recognise the limitations of general deterrence as a guide to sentencing policy. As an alternative, they stressed the role of punishment as a reinforcer of citizens' inhibitions against crime. The criminal sanction, the Norwegian penologist Johannes Andenaes thus has pointed out, is a 'concrete expression of society's disapproval' of criminal acts, and thereby 'creates conscious and unconscious inhibitions against crime'.[4]

This norm-reinforcing function is sometimes said to provide the basis for the principle of proportionality. A number of German legal theorists have contended, for example, that a penalty structure in which penalties were made commensurate with the gravity of crimes will be perceived as more just, and being so perceived, will better strengthen citizens' self-restraint and respect for law.[5] Disproportionate sanctions are said to risk weakening the moral influence of the penalty structure.

A possible response would be to treat the Bentham-Beccaria thesis as a *prophylactic* principle. In the absence of empirical data, we might construct scenarios of what could happen if (say) penalties for middle-level offences were raised to approach the severities imposed on serious crimes. If changes in sanction severity generally had little impact on crime rates, then there would be no such counterproductive effect of increased serious offending. If, however, sentence severity were to matter for deterrence, then counterproductive effects—of a switch to more serious offending—might occur. Since serious offending is so much more damaging, individually and socially, those consequences would be much more undesirable. For a fuller discussion of this scenario approach, see A von Hirsch, A Bottoms et al, *Criminal Deterrence and Sentence Severity: An Analysis of Recent Research* (Oxford, Hart Publishing, 1999) 41–43.

[4] J Andenaes, *Punishment and Deterrence* (Ann Arbor, Michigan, University of Michigan Press, 1982) 3–33.
[5] C Roxin, 'Zur jüngsten Diskussion über Schuld, Prävention und Verantwortlichkeit im Strafrecht' in A Kaufmann et al (eds), *Festschrift für Paul Bockelmann*

Plausible as this argument seems, it does not stand up well under closer scrutiny. The idea, ultimately, remains one of crime prevention. It involves the assertion that if one punishes proportionately, the citizenry's moral inhibitions against offending will be better reinforced, which in turn will enable the criminal law to carry out its crime-preventative role more successfully.

A question that naturally comes to mind is: how does one know? There is actually little evidence on how much punishment reinforces law-abiding attitudes.[6] If we understand so little about how and to what extent punishment reinforces conscientious self-restraint, that would be a frail basis for a policy of proportionate sanctions.

Even if better evidence was obtained, the argument from positive general prevention would still not be sustainable. It points to the supposed 'disappointment' of citizens' expectations of fairness that disproportionate sanctions would evoke, and the possibly resulting weakening of their inhibitions against criminal behaviour. There exists scant reason to believe, however, that citizens actually care much about the role of proportionality in sentencing law; or even if they did care, that they take sufficient notice of the specifics of sentencing doctrine to have their inhibitions against offending affected.[7] The argument also fails to account for our sense that sentence-proportionality is not just a prudential norm but an *ethical* principle. We feel there is something wrong, not simply counterproductive in the long run, about inflicting punishments that are not fairly commensurate with the gravity of offences. That sense of wrongfulness cannot be explained merely by arguing that proportionality influences citizens' attitudes in such a way as to reinforce their inclination towards law abidance.

(München, CH Beck, 1979) 304–07. However, Roxin has retreated from this view in subsequent writings; see, C Roxin, 'Prevention, Censure and Responsibility: The Recent Debate on the Purposes of Punishment' in AP Simester, A Du Bois-Pedain and U Neumann (eds), *Liberal Criminal Theory: Essays for Andreas von Hirsch* (Oxford, Hart Publishing, 2014) Ch 2. For critiques of the evidentiary and ethical basis of this positive-general-prevention argument, see B Schünemann, A von Hirsch and N Jareborg (eds), *Positive Generalprävention* (Heidelberg, CF Müller, 1998) 17–28, 83–100, 125–52.

[6] See KF Schumann, 'Empirische Beweisbarkeit der Grundannahmen von positiver Generalprävention' in Schünemann, von Hirsch and Jareborg 1998.

[7] W Frisch, 'Schwächen und berechtigte Aspekte der Theorie der positiven Generalprävention' in Schünemann, von Hirsch and Jareborg 1998.

4.3 THE ARGUMENT FROM CENSURE

The requirement of proportionate sentences does not, in my view, rest on such crime-prevention considerations. It is grounded directly, instead, on the notions of censure in punishment.

Punishing someone consists of doing something unpleasant to him, because he has purportedly committed a wrong, under circumstances and in a manner that conveys disapprobation of him for his wrong. The visitation of censure, as noted previously (Chapter 3), is a central justifying feature of punishment. If one asks why penalties ought to be levied proportionately to the gravity of the criminal conduct, therefore, the answer is not that this would improve crime-preventative effects, for it may or may not do so. The requirement of proportionate punishment should, instead, be derived directly from the censuring implications of the criminal sanction. Once one has created an institution with the condemnatory implications that punishment has, then it is a requirement of justice, not merely of efficient crime prevention, to punish offenders according to the degree of blameworthiness of their conduct. Disproportionate punishments are unjust not because they may be ineffectual or possibly counterproductive, but because these would purport to condemn the actor for his conduct and yet visit more disapprobation on him than the gravity of his conduct would warrant.

A few comments about this censure-based justification for proportionality are in order. It makes clear that the principle of proportionality in sentencing does not rest on factual claims that commensurability in punishment enhances the crime-preventive utility of the penal system. Suppose we were to discover evidence that proportionate punishments were no more effective a deterrent than (and perhaps not even as effective as) harsh, disproportionate ones. Suppose, further, that new psychological evidence suggested that formal penal sanctions, whether proportionate or not, contributed little to the development of people's inhibitions against offending. Would such evidence mean that we properly could ignore requirements of proportionality? Certainly not. As long as the state continues to respond to violence, theft, and other noxious conduct through the institution of the criminal sanction, it is treating those whom it punishes as wrongdoers and censuring them for their behaviour. If the sanction thus visits blame on offenders for their conduct, then the severity of the state's response ought as a matter of justice reflect the degree of blameworthiness, that is, the gravity, of actors' conduct.

This argument uses a commonly-understood concept, employed in everyday life as well as in criminal law: the notion of censure. The idea is that once a blaming institution has been established to respond to criminal acts, then its sanctions ought to be allocated in a manner that reflects its logic of censure, ie, that comports fairly with the degree of reprehensibility of those acts. The argument does not presuppose any talionic idea of requiting evil for evil, nor of other arcane notions that have surfaced in the literature of retribution.[8]

Andenaes has questioned whether this censure-based argument for proportionality is circular.[9] Punishment entails censure, he suggests, only in a system in which the severity of the sentence is tied to judgments about the degree of wrongfulness of the conduct. Were the system's rules for allocating sentencing more thoroughly utilitarian, he suggests, the link between punishing and blaming could well disappear. The nexus between punishment and blame, however, has deeper roots than the sentencing rules of the particular jurisdiction. Censure is integral to the very conception of punishing—as should be apparent from the earlier-cited illustration of the difference between a tax and a fine; and on a more theoretical level, from the censure-based account of punishment that has been sketched in the previous chapter.

4.4 THE CENSURE ARGUMENT STATED MORE FULLY

The argument in favour of the principle of proportionality is, in brief, the following: that since punishment does and should convey blame, its amount should reflect the degree of blameworthiness of the criminal conduct. But this argument needs to be articulated more fully.

---

[8] See discussion in ch 3, above.

[9] J Andenaes, 'Nyklassicisme, Proporsjonalitet og Prevensjon' (1988) *Nordisk Tidsskrift for Kriminalvidenskab* 75, 41; for a response, A von Hirsch and N Jareborg, 'Straff och Proportionalitet—Replik' (1989) *Nordisk Tidsskrift for Kiminalvidenskab* 76, 56.

Stated schematically, the case for proportionality in sentencing involves the following three steps:[10]

> *Step 1:* The State's sanctions against criminal conduct should take a punitive form; that is, visit deprivations in a manner that expresses censure or blame.
>
> *Step 2:* The comparative severity of a sanction expresses the stringency of the blame.
>
> *Step 3:* Hence, punitive sanctions should be arrayed according to the degree of blameworthiness (ie seriousness) of the conduct.

Let us examine each of these steps. Step (1) reflects the claim made in the previous chapter: that the response to the injurious conduct with which the criminal law deals should convey censure. A 'neutral' sanction embodying no disapprobation would not merely be a (possibly) less efficient preventive device; it would be objectionable on the ethical ground that it does not take cognisance the wrongfulness of the conduct, and does not treat the actor as a moral agent answerable for his or her behaviour.

Step (2) has also been addressed: that in punishment, deprivation or hard treatment is the vehicle for expressing censure. When a given type of conduct is visited with comparatively greater severity, it therefore signifies a greater degree of disapprobation.[11]

Step (3)—the conclusion—embodies the claim of fairness. When offenders are (and should be) dealt with through a sanction ascribing censure, their punishments should reflect how reprehensible their conduct can reasonably be characterised as being. By penalising one kind of conduct more severely than another, the punishing authority conveys the message that the conduct is worse—which is appropriate only if the conduct is indeed worse (ie more serious). If penalties were ordered in severity inconsistently with the comparative seriousness of crime, the less reprehensible conduct would, undeservedly, receive the greater reprobation.

---

[10] This scheme of argument was originally set forth in A von Hirsch, *Censure and Sanctions* (Oxford, Oxford University Press, 1993) 15–17.

[11] See discussion of the 'intertwining' of the censuring and preventive function in ch 3 above, and later in the present chapter. See also text accompanying nn 89–91.

The foregoing case for proportionality would be straightforward enough if censure was the sole warrant for punishment. But the justification for the existence of punishment which I have offered in the preceding chapter (Chapter 3) is a hybrid one, which relies on notions of crime prevention as well as censure. Does this create a Trojan Horse? If punishment's existence is justified even in part on the ground of crime prevention, might not that ground alone be invoked in deciding comparative severities of punishment? If that were permissible, the foregoing argument for sentence-proportionality would be undermined.[12]

If the two justifying elements, censure and prevention, were to operate separately on different features of the criminal sanction, this would become a problem. Suppose, for example, that one were to assert that the judgment of conviction represented censure of the offender, and the penalty then imposed performed only a preventive function. Then, the determination of the sanction's severity might be determined solely on preventive grounds, and proportionality requirements could be disregarded. Such a model, however, would be unacceptable, because if the penalty were to operate purely preventatively, instead expressing disapprobation for the offender's conduct, then this separate non-condemnatory response would clearly fall outside my proposed justification for punishment, outlined in the previous chapter. We would no longer be speaking of a censure-expressing response that, for supplementary preventive reasons, conveys its disapproval through material deprivation rather than purely symbolic means. Instead, the deprivation imposed on the offender would be simply preventive and not censure-

---

[12] An American penologist, D Dolinko, 'Three Mistakes about Retributivism' (1992) *University of Chicago Law Review* 39, 1623 has made this objection: if punishment has the twin objectives of censure and prevention, why not distribute punishments according to the latter aim? He then notes my reply: that censure is an essential characteristic of punishment, so that the comparative severity of the penalty will convey the degree of reprobation. His response is an odd one: tort liability, he asserts, in some sense conveys censure, since a prerequisite of liability ordinarily is fault on the part of the actor. Yet the amount of civil recovery depends not on fault but on what is required to compensate the plaintiff. Why, then, need fault be the sole measure for the quanta of punishments? The answer to Dolinko's argument should be obvious: civil remedies are chiefly designed to compensate, and do not have censure as a central defining feature as punishment does; see, further, A von Hirsch and A Ashworth, *Proportionate Sentencing: Exploring the Principles* (Oxford, Oxford University Press, 2005) 134–37.

based at all; it would be the 'beast control' kind that would not address the actor as a moral agent (see Chapter 3).

What is crucial about my suggested 'mixed' rationale, is the intertwining of punishment's censuring and hard treatment features. It is the penal deprivation, not just the judgment of conviction, that expresses the censure as well as serving as the prudential disincentive. Imposing a penal deprivation on the offender visits him with disapprobation that is justifiable only if he is at fault—which is why the fault-requirements of substantive criminal law should be observed.[13] Altering the amount of the penal deprivation will alter the stringency of the censure conveyed, and is warranted only where that would reflect an altered degree of blameworthiness (ie, the seriousness) of the criminal conduct—which is why the requirements of proportionality ought to be observed. Once this crucial feature of intertwining is understood, we need no longer fear a Trojan Horse.

A simple illustration can suggest why my bifurcated account would not permit comparative severities to be decided on preventive grounds. Consider a proposal to increase sanctions for a specified type of conduct (above the quantum that would be proportionate) in order to create a stronger disincentive against offending. Could such a step be justified under my theory of punishment—on grounds that prevention is deemed to be part of the general aim of punishing and that this measure could achieve prevention more efficiently? No, it would not, for the following reasons.

i. Suppose the increase were accomplished simply by raising the prescribed penalty for this type of crime. That increase in punishment would express increased disapprobation for conduct that, *ex hypothesi*, has become no more reprehensible. The increase thus would be objectionable because it treats the offender as more to blame than his conduct warrants.

ii. Alternatively, the increase might be accomplished by visiting the proportionate punishment, and then inflicting a separate *non-condemnatory* sanction. Since the additional imposition would not be reprobative in character, it would involve no unjustifiable increase in blame. There is, however, another objection: this additional non-condemnatory sanction clearly falls outside my

---

[13] See also von Hirsch and Ashworth 2005, 135–37.

proposed justification for the hard treatment. We would no longer be speaking of a censure-expressing sanction that, for preventive reasons, also involves material deprivation. Instead, the additional sanction is purely preventive and not reprobative at all. It is of the 'beast control' kind that would not address the actor as a moral agent (see Chapter 3 above).

These scenarios confirm what should be apparent, anyway: that making prevention part of the justification for punishment's existence, in the manner that I have suggested, does not permit it to operate independently as a basis for deciding comparative punishments. Any increase or decrease in the severity-ranking of a penalty on the penalty scale alters how much disapprobation is expressed—and hence needs to be justified by reference to the seriousness of the criminal conduct.

For further reading:

Ashworth, Andrew, and Lucia Zedner (2014) *Preventive Justice* (Oxford, Oxford University Press).

Frase, Richard S (2011) 'Can Above-Desert Penalties be Justified by Competing Deontological Theories?' in M Tonry, (ed), *Retributivism Has a Past. Has It a Future?* (New York, Oxford University Press) Ch 9.

Frase, Richard S (2011) 'Excessive Relative to What? Defining Constitutional Proportionality Principles' in M Tonry (ed), *Why Punish? How Much? A Reader on Punishment* (New York, Oxford University Press) Ch 17.

Steiker, Carol (2013) 'Proportionality as a Limit on Preventive Justice: Promises and Pitfalls' in A Ashworth, L Zedner and P Tomlin (eds), *Prevention and the Limits of the Criminal Law* (Oxford, Oxford University Press).

5

Ordinal and Cardinal Proportionality

MUCH OF THE debate over the idea of penal desert has concerned the extent to which it guides the choice of sanctions. Retributivists are said to assert that desert alone should determine the scaling of penalties. Others—including the late University of Chicago penologist Norval Morris—have disagreed, and claim that the concept of desert can provide no more than broad limits on penalty severity. My view is that the proper role of desert is actually more complex than either contention suggests.

Professor Morris's position is one he named 'limiting retributivism'—a mixed model somewhere between full retributivism and straightforward penal utilitarianism.[1] Desert, he contended, can supply only the approximate upper and lower bounds within which a penalty may justly be levied; within these bounds, crime-prevention aims (namely, incapacitative and rehabilitative considerations) should be decisive. Desert thus properly should serve merely as a limiting, not a determining principle. In Morris' words:

> Desert is not a defining principle; it is a limiting principle. The concept of 'just desert' sets the maximum and minimum of the sentence that may be imposed for any offence and helps to define the punishment relationships between offences; it does not give any more fine-tuning to the appropriate sentence than that. The fine-tuning is to be done on utilitarian principles.[2]

The reason desert is only limiting, Morris argues, is that none of us have an idea precisely how much punishment is deserved for any given

---

[1] N Morris, *Punishment, Desert, and Rehabilitation* (Washington, DC, US Government Printing Office, 1976); N Morris, *Madness and the Criminal Law* (Chicago, Chicago University Press, 1982).

[2] Morris 1982. For a recent analysis of Morris' views, see RS Frase, *Just Sentencing: Principles and Procedures for a Workable System* (New York, Oxford University Press, 2013) 11–12.

offence. We can only grasp what would be manifestly *dis*proportionate in lenience or severity.

Since desert is only a limit, Morris continues, the sentencer is not obligated to impose equally onerous sentences on equally deserving (or rather, undeserving) criminals. Cases that are alike in respect to the degree of blameworthiness of defendants' conduct may be treated unlike where called for by utilitarian ends—provided none of those disparate punishments become manifestly disproportionate to the degree of iniquity of the crime.

When one asks whether desert is limiting or determining, however, it is necessary to specify: *limiting or determining for what purpose?* It is essential, in particular, to distinguish between *ordinal* and *cardinal* magnitudes of punishment, that is, between the questions of (1) how severely crimes should be punished relative to each other, and (2) what overall degree of onerousness should characterise the system of penalties. To view desert as decisive for comparative punishments does not commit one to the claim that it is also determinative for deciding the overall magnitude and anchor-points of the penalty scale.[3]

For desert theory, this distinction is crucial. In deciding ordinal ranking of penalties, desert provides considerably more guidance than Norval Morris's thesis suggests. But desert provides a lesser degree of guidance (albeit some, I shall argue) in deciding the system's overall degree of punitiveness and its anchoring points. Let me explain.

5.1 ORDINAL PROPORTIONALITY

The issue of ordinal proportionality concerns how severely an offence should be punished compared to similar criminal acts, and compared to other crimes of greater or lesser seriousness. Its requirements are

---

[3] This distinction was one that I first set forth in A von Hirsch, *Past or Future Crimes: Deservedness and Dangerousness in the Sentencing of Criminals* (New Brunswick, New Jersey, Rutgers University Press, 1985) United Kingdom edn (Manchester: Manchester University Press, 1986)) Ch 4. For a later restatement, A von Hirsch and A Ashworth, *Proportionate Sentencing: Exploring the Principles* (Oxford, Oxford University Press, 2005) 137–43.

reasonably specific. Persons convicted of criminal acts of similar gravity should receive punishments of comparable severity. Persons convicted of crimes of dissimilar gravity should receive punishments correspondingly graded in their degree of onerousness. These requirements of ordinal proportionality are not mere limits, and they are infringed when persons found guilty of comparably reprehensible conduct receive substantially unequal sanctions on ulterior (eg crime-prevention) grounds. These ordinal proportionality requirements are readily explained on the censure-based conception of punishment outlined in the previous two chapters (3 and 4). Since punishing one type of offence more severely than another expresses greater disapprobation of the former, it is justified only to the extent that the former conduct is, indeed, more reprehensible.

This conception militates against resolving questions of comparative severities of sentence on grounds other than the degree of blameworthiness of the offender's conduct. It precludes, for example, punishing a particular burglar more severely than other convicted burglars not because his particular criminal conduct has been any worse, but because he represents a greater risk of returning to crime.

To disregard ordinal proportionality requirements, and treat desert as providing only the broad limits that Morris suggests, would disregard the censuring implications of punishment. Suppose one decides that, for a given type of crime, less than X months imprisonment is deemed undeservedly lenient, and more than Y months, undeservedly severe. Suppose one treats desert as supplying only those outer limits—that the sentence must fall somewhere between these wide bounds of X and Y—and then allows the disposition to be decided within these bounds chiefly on grounds of crime prevention. This would permit sentences of substantially differing severity to be imposed on offenders whose conduct is equally reprehensible but who, say, are considered to represent differing degrees of risk of recidivism. One offender may receive a punishment close to the lower limit, X, and another may get a sentence at the upper limit, Y. Through these divergent penalties, the two offenders would be visited with substantially different degrees of censure, although the blameworthiness of their conduct is much the same. In fact, a defendant who commits the less serious offence might receive the greater penalty comparatively, if (say) he is deemed to represent a sufficiently high risk of recidivism.

5.2 THE SUB-REQUIREMENTS OF ORDINAL
PROPORTIONALITY: PARITY AND RANK-ORDERING

Ordinal proportionality has two main sub-requirements. The first is *parity*: when offenders have been convicted of crimes of comparable seriousness, they deserve penalties of comparable severity. This does not necessarily call for imposition of the same penalty for all acts within a statutory crime category—as significant variations may occur within that category in the conduct's degree of harmfulness or culpability. But once such within-category variations in crime-seriousness are taken into account, the resulting penalties should have substantially the same degree of onerousness. (This parity requirement has one major exception, concerning the role of prior convictions that will be discussed in Chapter 7 below).

A second sub-requirement is *rank-ordering*. Punishing crime Y more severely than crime X expresses greater disapprobation for crime Y, which is warranted only if it is significantly more serious. Punishments thus should be ordered on the scale of penalties so that their relative severity reflects the seriousness-ranking of the crimes involved.

Because of these two ordinal-proportionality constraints, proportionality provides considerably more guidance than Norval Morris's view of desert-as-mere-limits suggests. The constraints, however, are not wholly 'determinative': they do not impose a unique set of solutions on how much any offence given should be punished. Within two penalty systems of differing overall levels of punitiveness, an offence may well receive a differing quanta of punishments.

5.3 HOW MUCH DOES ORDINAL PROPORTIONALITY
CONSTRAIN RELIANCE ON CRIME-PREVENTION CONCERNS?

To what extent do ordinal proportionality requirements restrict the pursuit of crime prevention in determining the sentence? That depends on whether or not the particular crime prevention strategy would call for substantial inequalities in the punishments imposed on those whose criminal conduct is comparably serious. Consider the strategy of predictively-based incapacitation: those forecasted to be higher risks are to receive longer prison sentences, to restrain them from reoffending. As predictions of risk of recidivism depend chiefly on factors that are not related to crime-seriousness (most notably, the offender's previous criminal history),[4] utilising such factors to decide the severity of sentence would infringe upon the parity requirements of ordinal proportionality. Not all crime prevention strategies, however, require such inequalities. Rehabilitation, for example, may not do so in some circumstances. Consider, for example, those convicted of serious crimes and sent to prison. If, among such persons, those deemed amenable to treatment are selected for enrolment in rehabilitative programmes during a specified portion of their prison sentence, this ordinarily would not substantially affect the onerousness of their punishment and hence would involve no breach of parity requirements. Ordinal proportionality is, likewise, observed when a choice is made among comparably severe non-custodial penalties on rehabilitative grounds—as will be discussed more fully in Chapter 8, below. Crime control may be invoked in deciding the comparative severity of sentence, in other words, when this would not disturb the proportionate ordering of punishments.

5.4 CARDINAL MAGNITUDE AND THE FIXING OF THE PENALTY SYSTEM'S ANCHORING POINTS

Once penalties have been graded according to the comparative seriousness of crimes, the penalty system as a whole still needs to be anchored. This is the issue of cardinal magnitude. It is here that desert must play a more restricted role.

The reason why this is so is the greater imprecision of cardinal desert judgements. Suppose one is trying to find the appropriate, deserved penalty for the offence of residential burglary. If one has already decided the penalties for certain other crimes, then one can locate the burglary penalty by making comparative judgements: how much more or less serious is a typical burglary (or typical burglary of a certain subtype) than those other crimes? But such judgements require a starting point, and the issue of cardinal magnitude deals with finding that starting point. There seems to be no crime for which one can readily

---

[4] AE Bottoms and A von Hirsch, 'The Crime-Preventive Impact of Penal Sanctions' in P Cane and HM Kritzer (eds), *The Oxford Handbook of Empirical Legal Studies* (Oxford, Oxford University Press, 2010) Ch 4, 114–17.

perceive a specific quantum of punishment as the uniquely deserved one.

This intuition is confirmed when one considers the conception of censure that underlies proportionalist sentencing theory. Assessments of ordinal proportionality rest on judgements of comparative blameworthiness. When judged in absolute rather than comparative terms, however, the censure expressed through penal deprivation is in part a convention, expressing a degree of disapprobation of criminal conduct through a given degree of onerousness of penalties. When the scale of penalties has been devised to reflect the comparative gravity of crimes, altering the scale's overall degree of punitiveness by making *pro rata* upward or downward changes in all prescribed sanctions would represent a change in that convention.

This ordinal-cardinal distinction helps resolve the difficulties of specifying deserved penalties under a desert model, mentioned at the outset of this chapter. The leeway which desert allows in fixing the penalty scale's overall degree of onerousness explains why we cannot identify a single right or fitting penalty for a crime. Whether X months, Y months, or somewhere in between is the appropriate penalty for a given type of offence depends on how the scale of penalties has been anchored and what punishments are prescribed for other, more and less serious crimes. Once those anchoring points are decided, however, the more restrictive requirements of ordinal proportionality apply. This would militate against giving long prison terms to some of those convicted for a given type of crime, and giving shorter prison terms to others, on the basis of (say) predictive factors not reflecting the degree of seriousness of the criminal conduct.

5.5 HOW MUCH GUIDANCE REGARDING ANCHORING OF THE PENALTY STRUCTURE?

Does this purported solution leave the anchoring of the scale of penalties too wide open? Could it permit a very severe system of penalties, so long as it is not so harsh as to impose drastic sanctions on manifestly trivial crimes? I think not.

To see why not, let us begin with a hypothetical scale of penalties which is ordered internally according to ordinal proportionality requirements, and which approximates in its overall degree of onerousness that of existing penalty levels. If the censure expressed through differing overall levels of penal deprivation is in part a matter of convention, as just suggested, then a plausible place to begin would be with the existing conventions regarding severity. The issue then would arise whether those norms should be altered—either in the direction of increased overall penalty levels, or in the direction of across-the-board penalty reductions. Desert theorists, including Andrew Ashworth and myself, have argued in favour of the latter: penalty levels should not be increased compared with existing practice, and should, where feasible, be scaled downward. What kind of arguments could be made in support of this view?[5]

One kind of argument draws on moral claims that extend beyond desert theory, and concerns the additional suffering that high overall levels of punitiveness would inflict on convicted offenders.[6] Expanded reliance on imprisonment, particularly longer-term imprisonment, would have devastating effects on those incarcerated. Such added suffering cannot be justified on grounds that offenders deserve it, for reasons already made clear: on a proportionalist, censure-orientated rationale, there exists considerable leeway in setting the overall severity levels of a penalty scale. A system of moderate sanctions could perform the censuring function as well as a harsher system.

High overall severity levels would, moreover, be inconsistent with the moral functions of penal censure discussed earlier (Chapter 3). Through punishment's censuring features, the criminal sanction provides a normative reason for desistance that can be offered to human beings viewed as moral agents: that doing certain acts is wrong and hence should be eschewed. The material deprivations of punishment can then be viewed as providing a supplemental disincentive—as providing citizens (given human fallibility and the temptations of offending) with additional prudential reason for compliance. The higher

---

[5] A Ashworth, *Sentencing and Criminal Justice*, 6th edn (Cambridge, Cambridge University Press, 2015) Ch 4; von Hirsch and Ashworth 2005, Ch 9; see also, G Roebuck and D Wood, 'A Retributive Argument against Punishment' (2011) *Criminal Law & Philosophy* 5, 73.

[6] For a fuller discussion of this question, see A von Hirsch, *Censure and Sanctions* (Oxford, Oxford University Press, 1993) Ch 5. That chapter also addresses the question whether and to what extent, if empirical data were available, crime-control aims could be considered in setting anchoring points.

penalty levels rise, however, the less significant the normative reasons for desistence supplied by penal censure would become, and the more predominant the system's purely threatening aspects would be—that is, the more the system would become, in Hegel's apt words, 'a stick raised to a dog'. This argument points towards keeping penalties at moderate levels: towards restraint in the use of severe sentences.[7]

How much guidance will this theory give? The model, admittedly, provides only a limited degree of guidance on the setting of the penalty system's anchoring points—that is, the penal system's overall degrees of punitiveness. But it provides considerably more guidance (albeit not providing unique solutions) regarding the comparative scaling of penalties. Desert theory thus can provide considerably more structure than Norval Morris's thesis, with which we began this chapter, conceded.[8]

For further reading:

Frase, Richard S (2013) *Just Sentencing: Principles and Procedures for a Workable System* (New York, Oxford University Press).

Lippke, Richard L (2012) 'Anchoring the Sentencing Scale: A Modest Proposal' *Theoretical Criminology* 16, 463.

Robinson, Paul H (2008) *Distributive Principles of Criminal Law: Who Should Be Punished How Much?* (Oxford, Oxford University Press).

Ryberg, Jesper (2007) *The Ethics of Proportionate Punishment: A Critical Investigation* (Dordrecht, Kluwer Academic Publishers).

---

[7] Ibid 42–46; and for interesting sceptical questions, see M Matravers, 'Is Twenty-First Century Punishment Post-Desert?' in M Tonry (ed), *Retributivism Has a Past: Has it a Future?* (New York, Oxford University Press, 2011) Ch 2.

[8] See ch 10, section 10.6 below for further discussion of anchoring points.

6

Seriousness, Severity and the Living-standard

THE PRINCIPLE OF proportionality requires the *severity* of penalties to be decided chiefly by reference to the *seriousness* of crimes. Therefore, we need a way of assessing each of the two elements, of crime-seriousness and punishment-severity. Suppose someone proposes that crime X be visited by punishment Y. In order to tell whether this is a proportionate sanction, one needs first to be able to judge how reprehensible crime X is compared to other crimes, and also how onerous penalty Y would be compared to other penalties.

6.1 GAUGING CRIMES' SERIOUSNESS

Ordinary people, several opinion surveys have found, show considerable consensus about the comparative seriousness of crimes.[1] Sentencing-guidelines commissions also have been able to rank crimes in comparative gravity, for purposes of devising numerical guidelines for sentencing—without encountering great disagreement among their members.[2] While the grading task proved time-consuming, it did not generate much dissensus within the commissions.

---

[1] A series of empirical studies have assessed public perceptions of the seriousness of offences, beginning with Thorsten Sellin's and Marvin Wolfgang's classic study *The Measurement of Delinquency* (New York, John Wiley, 1964). These studies provide respondents surveyed with brief descriptions of various criminal incidents, and ask them to rate the seriousness of the offences described. The studies suggest that persons from differing walks of life tend to rank offences similarly. For a review of recent research, see S Stylianou, 'Measuring Crime Seriousness Perceptions: What Have We Learned and What Else Do We Want to Know' (2003) *Journal of Criminal Justice* 31, 37.

[2] A von Hirsch, K Knapp and M Tonry, *The Sentencing Commission and its Guidelines* (Boston, Northeastern University Press, 1987) 96–101; see also, RS Frase, *Just Sentencing: Principles and Procedures for a Workable System* (New York, Oxford University Press, 2013) Ch 3.

Less developed, however, has been the state of the theory. What criteria should be used for assessing and ranking crimes' gravity? The seriousness of a crime depends upon the degree of risked harmfulness of the conduct, and the extent of the actor's culpability. Culpability can be gauged with the aid of clues from the substantive criminal law. The substantive law distinguishes intentional conduct from reckless and from criminally negligent behaviour.[3] It should be possible to develop, for sentencing doctrine, more refined distinctions concerning the degree of purposefulness, indifference to consequences, or carelessness in criminal conduct. The doctrines of excuse in the substantive criminal law could also be drawn upon to develop norms concerning partial excuse—for example, of partial duress, and diminished capacity.[4]

The harm dimension of seriousness is less easy to assess, however, because substantive law provides few clues: the law does not formally distinguish crimes' degrees of harmfulness in systematic fashion. How, then, can one compare the injuriousness of acts that invade different interests: say, compare crime X that intrudes upon property interests with crime Y that chiefly affects personal privacy?

A theory of harm that relies on measures of quality of life may help answer that question, and such a theory has been sketched by Nils Jareborg and I in a 1991 essay.[5] According to our theory, victimising harms should be ranked in seriousness according to how much they typically would affect a person's *standard of living*. We use that term in the broad sense suggested by the Harvard economist and philosopher Amartya Sen,[6] which reflects both economic and non-economic interests.

The living standard is one of a family of related notions, including wellbeing, that refer to the quality of persons' lives. Wellbeing, however, can be highly personalised: one's life quality depends on one's particular focal aims; to the person who wants to devote his life to contemplation and prayer, for example, material comfort and ordinary social amenities

---

[3] See, eg, American Law Institute, Model Penal Code (1962), s 2.02 (2).

[4] A von Hirsch and A Ashworth, *Proportionate Sentencing: Exploring the Principles* (Oxford, Oxford University Press, 2005) 186–87.

[5] A von Hirsch and N Jareborg, 'Gauging Criminal Harm: A Living-Standard Analysis' (1991) *Oxford Journal of Legal Studies* 11, 1.

[6] A Sen, *The Standard of Living* (Cambridge, Cambridge University Press, 1987); A Sen, Amartya (2009). *The Idea of Justice* (Cambridge, Massachusetts, Harvard University Press, 2009) Chs 11–14.

may matter little. However, the living standard, in Sen's sense, does not focus on individual life-quality or goal achievement, but on the *means or capabilities* for achieving a certain quality of life. Some of these means are material (shelter and financial resources) but others are not so (eg personal privacy). The living-standard, in Sen's sense, is also standardised, referring to the means and capabilities that would *ordinarily* promote a good life. Someone has a good standard of living, according to this perspective, if he has the health, material resources and other means that people ordinarily can utilise to have good lives.

Using the living-standard as a way of gauging harms has a number of advantages. First, it seems to fit the way we usually judge harms. Why is aggravated assault considered more harmful than burglary? It is because the quality of the person's life—in the sense of his living resources—has been more adversely affected. Second, the living-standard idea permits drawing from a rich array of experience— including experience outside of the criminal law. We can ask how the harm in an arson attack compares with that in an accidental fire. Finally, a living-standard analysis would allow for cultural variation. Differing living-arrangements in different societies can affect the consequences of criminal acts, and normative differences among cultures can affect the impact of those consequences on the quality of persons' lives. The harmfulness of residential burglary, for example, depends on the degree to which a private home is ordinarily the focal point for people's everyday existence; and on the degree to which privacy is valued in a particular culture. A living-standard analysis thus could, in another culture, lead to a different rating for burglary—if the home has a different social role and if a different valuation is given to privacy.

Jareborg's and my suggested analysis begins with parcelling out the various kinds of interests that offences typically involve. After the interests involved in a given type of offence are thus identified, their importance may be judged by assessing their significance with reference to the living standard.[7]

Most victimising offences affect one or more of the following interest-dimensions: (1) physical integrity, (2) material resources, (3) privacy,

---

[7] See also more recently, VA Greenfield and Letizia Paoli, 'A Framework to Assess the Harms of Crimes' (2013) *British Journal of Criminology* 53, 864 on gauging the degree of harmfulness of various kinds of criminal conduct.

and (4) dignity (eg freedom from humiliation). A simple residential burglary, for example, chiefly affects a person's material resources and privacy. The material loss would consist of what is stolen or damaged, plus the inconvenience and expense of repairs. The privacy-loss consists of the intrusion of a stranger into one's living-space. To rate the harmfulness of the conduct, the living-standard criterion should be applied to each dimension, successively. In the case of the burglary, the analysis would thus begin with its material-resources dimension. Here, the impact on the living standard may well be relatively modest: not much is stolen or destroyed in a typical burglary, so that a standard victim's material wellbeing would not be greatly affected. Next, the privacy dimension would be considered. Here, the rating should be higher, given the importance of privacy to a good existence, and the extent to which an intrusion into the home typically interferes with someone's privacy. The attraction of this mode of analysis is that each dimension involved—physical integrity, material resources, privacy, etc—can ultimately be assessed in terms of a common criterion: that of the impact on the living standard. This means that, in the burglary, one can compare the living-standard impact of the material loss (typically, rather limited) with that of the privacy-intrusion (significantly greater). One could also compare a burglary with other victimising offences involving different interests: say, an aggravated assault, where physical integrity and personal dignity (viz freedom from humiliation) are chiefly involved.

To aid in this analysis, the living-standard itself can be graded. One might make use of at least four living-standard levels: (1) subsistence, (2) minimal wellbeing, (3) marginally 'adequate' wellbeing, and (4) standard wellbeing. The first, subsistence, refers to survival but with maintenance of no more than elementary human capacities to function—in other words, barely getting by. The remaining levels refer to various degrees of life quality above that of mere subsistence. The function of these gradations is to provide a rough measure of the extent to which a typical criminal act intrudes upon the living standard. To take an obvious example, aggravated assault threatens subsistence, and thus does much more harm than a substantial theft—that, at worst, still leaves the person with at least an adequate level of comfort and dignity.

This analysis is helpful chiefly in gauging the standard harm involved in various categories or subcategories of offence. The point is to assess the injuriousness of typical instances of (say) residential burglary, or residential burglary of a certain kind (one might, for example, distinguish simple burglary from ransacking). It is not to gauge the injury done to an individual, John Jones, when his apartment has been broken into and his favourite sporting trophy has been stolen. The living-standard relates, as we noted, to the *standardised* means or capabilities for a good life—not to the life-quality of particular persons. Deviations from such standardised assessments should be made only in certain kinds of special circumstances, where the differences from the ordinary case are plainly apparent.

This harms analysis is no formula providing ready answers, because the impact of a crime on a person's living-standard is itself very much a matter of factual and normative judgement. It is also helpful mainly in addressing crimes directly affecting natural persons, rather than crimes involving collective interests.[8] The analysis nevertheless should be helpful as a guide to thinking about rating harms. Some attempts have also been made to apply the analysis in the contexts of Swedish, English, and German law.[9]

6.2 GAUGING PUNISHMENTS' SEVERITY

Grading penalties presupposes an ability to assess those sanctions' comparative severity. While prison sanctions (as noted earlier) may be compared by their duration, non-custodial sanctions' onerousness depends on their intensity as well. Three days of community service seems tougher than three days' probation.

A number of studies have attempted to measure sanction severity through opinion surveys. A selected group of respondents is shown a list of penalties of various kinds, and asked to rate their severity

---

[8] Nils Jareborg and I in our 1991 article (von Hirsch and Jareborg 1991), did attempt to apply the living-standard analysis to the latter kind of crimes, but we were less than satisfied with that aspect of our analysis. The issue requires further exploration.

[9] For an exploration of how the living-standard idea may be applied in Swedish sentencing law, see P Asp and A von Hirsch, 'Straffvärde' (1999) *Svensk Juristtidning* 151; for application of the idea to English law, see A Ashworth, *Sentencing and Criminal Justice*, 6th edn (Cambridge, Cambridge University Press, 2015) Ch 4; and to German law, see T Hörnle, *Tatproportionale Strafzumessung* (Berlin, Duncker und Humblot, 1999) 226–44.

on a numerical rating scale. The surveys tend to show a degree of consensus.[10] Such research, however, does not elucidate what is meant by severity; elicit respondents' reasons for their rankings; or assess the plausibility of those reasons. It is necessary to consider what *should* be the basis of comparing penalties—ie, to develop a theory for gauging punishments' severity.

A possible theory of severity would be that it depends upon how unpleasant the sanction typically is experienced as being. On this view, opinion surveys would be a useful way of assessing penalties, as these would reflect how onerous various penalties are perceived as being. Unpleasantness or discomfort is ultimately subjective: a matter of how various deprivations are typically experienced. If penalty Q is experienced as being more unpleasant than penalty R, this simply makes it so.[11]

Such a subjectivist conception of severity would have troublesome implications, however. It would permit a high degree of variation among offenders subjected to similar penal regimes. Some convicted persons are tough, others are tender, so that greater deprivations might possibly be visited on the tough ones, on grounds that they would feel them less keenly. This would also have troublesome social implications, to the extent that toughness and being accustomed to deprivation relate to social class.

The subjectivist approach seems also misconceived in principle. What makes punishments more or less onerous is not any identifiable sensation; rather, it is the degree to which those sanctions interfere with the vital interests of those punished. The severity of intensive probation supervision, for example, depends not on its 'feeling bad' in any immediate sense, but on its impinging upon such interests as being in charge of one's own life or moving about as one chooses.

It would thus seem helpful to apply an interests-analysis comparable to the one just suggested for gauging crime-seriousness. The more important the person's interests intruded upon by a sanction are, according to this perspective, the severer the penalty would be. Penalties could be ranked according to the degree to which they typically affect such interests as offenders' freedom of movement, earning

---

[10] See, eg, L Sebba and G Nathan, 'Further Exploration of the Scaling of Penalties' (1984) *British Journal of Criminology* 24, 221.

[11] See AJ Kolber, 'The Subjective Experience of Punishment' (2009) *Columbia Law Review* 109, 182.

ability, and so forth. The importance of those interests could then be gauged according to how they typically impinge on the *living-standard*—in the sense described earlier in this chapter. Such an interest-analysis also fits the way we discuss punishment severity. When asked to explain why long-term imprisonment is a severe sanction, for example, we would naturally answer in terms of how drastically its deprivations impinge on someone's quality of life.

Adopting an interest-analysis approach means that the assessment of severity is made less dependent on the preferences of particular individuals. The living-standard, as noted earlier, refers to the means and capabilities that *ordinarily* assist persons in achieving a good life. If a given interest is important in this sense to a good existence, it would warrant a high rating—notwithstanding that some persons might not much mind going without it. Imprisonment qualifies as a severe penalty, because of the interests in freedom of movement and privacy which it takes away are ordinarily so vital to a decent existence—even if a few defendants might happen to be claustrophiliacs. This helps answer an objection that sometimes has been raised to desert theory: namely, that one never can grade penalties' onerousness, because people's subjective perceptions of the onerousness of punishment supposedly are so varied.[12]

For further reading:

Bagaric, Mirko (2014) 'Proportionality in Sentencing: The Need to Factor in Community Experience, Not Public Opinion' in Jesper Ryberg and Julian V Roberts (eds), *Popular Punishment: On the Normative Significance of Public Opinion* (New York, Oxford University Press).

Markel, Dan, and C Flanders (2010) 'Bentham on Stilts: The Bare Relevance of Subjectivity to Retributive Justice' *California Law Review* 98, 907.

Robinson, Paul H and R Kurzban (2006) 'Concordance and Conflict in Intuitions of Justice' *Minnesota Law Review* 91, 1829.

Ryan, Meghan (2011) 'Proximate Retribution' *Houston Law Review* 48, 1049.

---

[12] For a statement of this objection, see N Walker, *Why Punish?* (Oxford, Oxford University Press, 1991).

7

The Role of Previous Convictions

IN TRADITIONAL DISCRETIONARY sentencing systems, judges typically adjusted the sentence to take account of the offender's previous convictions. However, the weight that should be given to the prior criminal record was uncertain. Should the defendant's criminal record be the primary determinant of the sentence? Or should the sentence chiefly reflect the seriousness of the current crime, with a limited adjustment made for the person's previous convictions? Under a discretionary system, different judges answered such questions differently. As jurisdictions move towards more explicit guidance for sentencing decisions, however, it becomes essential to decide how much weight the criminal record should have, and why.

The question has no simple answers. One sometimes hears it asserted, for example, that the criminal record should not be taken into account at all, because the offender has been 'punished already' for his previous crime. However, this reasoning is circular. If some feature of the offender having been previously convicted affects the rationale for his present punishment, then adjusting his sentence is not penalising him twice for his past crime. If, for example, the defendant has received a discount in the penalty for his first offence, removing or reducing that discount if he subsequently reoffends would not be punishing him twice over.

The significance of the prior criminal record will vary, depending on what sentencing rationale is being relied upon. A rationale emphasising prediction and incapacitation would give the record primary weight. Prediction studies generally show that the statistical likelihood of an offender reoffending is correlated chiefly with his previous criminal history, rather than with the seriousness of his current criminal act. What predicts recidivism best (or rather, least unreliably) is the offender's record of previous arrests (especially, early arrests) and convictions, plus certain facts about his social history, such as drug use and lack of regular employment.[1]

For present purposes, however, I am assuming a desert rationale, according to which punishments should be proportionate to the seriousness of the defendant's criminal conduct. On that rationale, what should the role of the criminal record be? There has been disagreement on this subject among desert theorists. One school of thought holds that the prior record should not be considered at all.[2] Another favours a theory of 'progressive loss of mitigation'.[3] According to this theory, the offender who is convicted for the first time should receive a discount in the penalty, but that discount should gradually diminish with subsequent reconvictions—so that after a certain number of reconvictions, it is lost entirely. Thereafter, the criminal record would call for no further adjustment. The discount, on this theory, should also be limited in magnitude—so that the seriousness of the offender's current crime, rather than the extent of his criminal record, would primarily determine the onerousness of the penalty.

I support this latter view. The offender should be punished less when he is first convicted; but with subsequent convictions, the discount should progressively diminish. The present chapter addresses *why* this should be the approach. The explanation needs to be one that comports with conceptions of desert—notably, with the censure-based conceptions addressed in this volume.

---

[1] National Academy of Sciences, Panel on Research on Criminal Careers, *Criminal Careers and 'Career Criminals'* in A Blumstein, J Cohen, J Roth and C Visher (Washington DC, National Academies of Sciences Press, 1986) Vol 1; AE Bottoms and A von Hirsch, 'The Crime-Preventive Impact of Penal Sanctions' in P Cane and HM Kritzer (eds), *The Oxford Handbook of Empirical Legal Studies* (Oxford, Oxford University Press, 2010) Ch 4, 114–17.

[2] G Fletcher, *Rethinking Criminal Law* (Boston, Little-Brown, 1978) 460–66; T Hörnle, *Tatproportionale Strafzumessung* (Berlin, Duncker und Humblot, 1999) 164–66.

[3] M Wasik, 'Guidelines, Guidance and Criminal Record' in M Wasik and K Pease (eds), *Sentencing Reform: Guidance or Guidelines?* (Manchester, Manchester University Press, 1987) Ch 7; A Ashworth, *Sentencing and Criminal Justice*, 6th edn (Cambridge, Cambridge University Press, 2015) Ch 6; A von Hirsch, 'Proportionality and the Progressive Loss of Mitigation: Some Further Reflections' in A von Hirsch and JV Roberts (eds), *Previous Convictions at Sentencing: Theoretical and Applied Perspectives* (Oxford, Hart Publishing, 2010) Ch 1.

7.1 EXPLANATIONS DIRECTED TO THE PRESENT ACT

Might the fact of a prior conviction or convictions alter the seriousness of the current crime? To do so, the prior offence would have to affect the harm or the culpability involved in the offender's current conduct. The harmfulness of his criminal conduct for which he is now being punished could not be affected. Obviously, the conduct's direct consequences or risks are unaltered. Conceivably, it could be argued that there is something akin to 'harm' involved—namely defiance: the repeat offender is seen as flouting the law, when he reoffends after having been punished already. But as Nils Jareborg has rightly pointed out, in a liberal society defiance should not be deemed a wrong that justifiably enhances what an offender deserves.[4] Treating defiance in itself as an extra 'harm' presupposes authoritarian assumptions about the state and the criminal law.

What about the offender's culpability of his current offence? In my 1976 volume, I did claim that his culpability was affected.[5] Before the defendant has been convicted, I argued, the offender is simply part of the general audience to whom the legal prohibition is addressed. He may not have paid the prohibition much attention, or understood its scope. The censure embodied in the punishment for the first offence, however, serves as a dramatic way of bringing the wrongfulness of the conduct to the actor's attention. Thereafter, claims on his part of possible ignorance or inattention to the prohibition become progressively less plausible.

I have since become convinced, however, that this argument is mistaken.[6] Granted, in some instances, a first offender may not have been fully aware of the prohibition or understood its scope or applicability. Even though most jurisdictions restrict the excusing effects of ignorance of law, sentencing theory might give such ignorance (or partial ignorance) greater culpability-reducing effect. However, many of those

---

[4] N Jareborg, 'Ideology and Crime: Basic Conceptions of Crime and their Implications' in R Lahti and K Nuotio (eds), *Criminal Law in Transition: Finnish and Comparative Perspectives* (Helsinki, Finnish Lawyers' Publishing Co, 1992); G Fletcher, 'The Recidivist Premium' (1982) *Criminal Justice Ethics* 1(2), 54, 57.

[5] A von Hirsch, *Doing Justice: The Choice of Punishments* (New York, Hill and Wang, Reprinted 1986 (Boston, Northeastern University Press, 1976)) Ch 10.

[6] See A von Hirsch, 'Desert and Previous Convictions in Sentencing' (1981) *Minnesota Law Review* 65, 591; von Hirsch 2010.

convicted for the first time would be well aware of the prohibition and of the wrongfulness of the act, but simply repeated the crime anyway. Ignorance, or failure to fully understand or take notice, does not support a generally applicable discount for first offenders.

7.2 EXPLANATIONS DIRECTED TO THE CRIMINAL CAREER

Why not look, instead, to the offender's criminal career? There are contexts in everyday life where we address the merit or demerit of a person's career as a whole. An example of career-desert is provided by prizes for distinguished research that learned societies periodically offer. Candidates' names, resumes and writings go to a panel of experts; after due deliberation, the panel chooses for the award one or more individuals whose scholarly output as a whole is thought to show the greatest distinction.

Such judgements, however, have a different logic than that employed in the criminal law. The prize is not *for* any particular work, but relates to the recipient's whole output. Nominees are not (as they are in essay competitions) required to submit any new product. The candidate's most recent efforts may be given little weight or be discounted entirely by judges, if his or her earlier contributions are considered to be more significant.

The criminal law is structured otherwise. The actor is punished for a particular crime—that for which he now stands convicted. The substantive criminal law defines, classifies, and prohibits *crimes*. (A career-oriented system would classify *persons* according to the frequency and gravity of their offending. It would make habitual offender laws the archetype of the criminal law, rather than its exception.) Existing trial and sentencing procedures are designed to determine the defendant's guilt or innocence for the current crime and to evaluate extenuating and aggravating circumstances surrounding that crime. Without drastic procedural changes, however, the criminal process does not have the means to inquire into the degree of demerit of a person's entire criminal career with care and discrimination.[7]

[7] Evaluating a criminal's 'career-desert' would call for in-depth information about past crimes for which he was convicted. One would, for example, need information about any aggravating or mitigating circumstances that had been found

Would it be desirable, however, to reshape the criminal law so as to emphasise criminal careers rather than crimes? I think not. The advantage of a criminal and sentencing law that focuses on crimes is that it provides a comprehensible valuation of conduct. What chiefly counts is the defendant's present criminal act in the case before the sentencing judge. The penal sanction thus can furnish a reasonably clear public expression of the degree of blameworthiness of that conduct.

A career-based system would make the law's public valuation of conduct much more diffuse. The focus would no longer be on what has now been done, but rather, on who did it and how frequently he did it before. It is true that the law's rules or principles would have to rate the gravity of crimes in order to set standards for criminal careers. But the punishment—the public expression of penal censure that is the product of such reckonings—would vary independently of the gravity of the current act, depending on the defendant's prior criminal record. As a result, the criminal sanction could no longer testify to the recognition of the wrongfulness of the conduct for which the offender is being sentenced, and to the significance of the rights that have been infringed.

7.3 AN ALTERNATIVE ACCOUNT: 'TOLERANCE' AND THE PRIOR RECORD

Further reflection has convinced me to approach this issue differently, beginning with a 1981 article.[8] The discount for the first offender, I have argued, should not rest on claims of lack of full knowledge or appreciation of the prohibition; it is, rather, a concession we should make to the fallibility of human nature. The reduced response for the first offence serves to accord some respect for the fact that the person's moral inhibitions functioned before, and to show some sympathy for the all-too-human fallibility that can lead to a first offence. The idea is thus one of a limited tolerance for human frailty.

Notice that we have this tolerance only because we have certain expectations, or should have them, about human beings and their

to exist with respect to any such previous crimes. Existing sentencing procedures and record-keeping methods are not remotely capable of establishing such facts.

[8] von Hirsch 1981; see more fully and recently, von Hirsch 2010.

nature. If we were angels, we would not require it. Were we sufficiently puritanical about humans, we would also deny the discount: human frailty, on that view, would be something to be abominated and confronted with vigour. But because humans are not angels, and should not be judged as though they were, a certain tolerance seems appropriate.

But how, precisely, does the notion of human fallibility link with notions of censure and desert? And if one wishes to be so tolerant, why not continue giving discounts even after numerous previous convictions? Since it also seems to be a fact of human nature that some people keep on reoffending, why not continue to grant further discounts even to multiple repeaters?

Our everyday moral judgements include the notion of a *lapse*. A transgression (even one of a substantial nature) is judged less stringently when it occurs against a background of prior compliance. The idea is that even an ordinarily well-behaved person can have his or her moral inhibitions fail in a moment of weakness or wilfulness. Such a loss of self-discipline is the kind of human frailty for which some understanding should be shown.

In sentencing, the lapse of which we are speaking is not just any moral failure, but an infringement of the standards of the criminal law. And the prior compliance in question is that of not having previously committed and been convicted for a criminal offence. It is not the offender's whole moral life that would be the subject of inquiry, but only his criminal record.[9] The logic of the first-offender discount, however, remains that of dealing with a lapse somewhat more tolerantly.

---

[9] Empirical research does suggest that, for each previous crime for which they were officially apprehended and punished, many offenders admit having committed several additional unpunished offences; see, eg, J Petersilia, P Greenwood and M Lavin, *Criminal Careers of Habitual Felons* (Santa Monica, California, RAND Corporation, 1977) 15–18. The vicissitudes of being discovered, arrested, prosecuted, and convicted are such that the absence of a record of criminal convictions is not a reliable indicator of whether a defendant has in fact previously committed crimes. But it would be unjust—and in many cases simply be inaccurate—to impute prior criminality to a defendant facing his first conviction on the basis of such statistical information about the presumed behaviour of other offenders. To deny a defendant the benefits of first-offender status, the sentencer should have proof that he actually was guilty of previous crimes and had been convicted and punished for them. The one safe proof that he was guilty should be a conviction for such crimes. The one formal mode of censure in the criminal law should be the imposition of a sentence for those crimes following conviction.

The muted disapprobation that the actor gets through the scaled-down penalty for his first conviction is still censure. It confronts the actor with the wrongfulness of the conduct and conveys disapprobation for that conduct. That remonstrance should give the person the opportunity to reconsider, reflect on the propriety of his conduct, and decide to pursue a different course. This is not a matter of giving the actor notice that the act was wrong, for he may well have been aware of that already. His offence may have been the result not of ignorance, but of having momentarily placed his own needs or inclinations above the requirements of respecting others' rights. But fallible humans are capable of thus acting, and the censure expressed through the prior punishment gives the person the opportunity to reflect on his misconduct.

Why, then, should we scale down the condemnatory and punitive response initially? It is because it is assumed that humans are both fallible and capable of doing something worthy of respect (namely, attending to censure). The fallibility calls for a limited tolerance of failure, expressed through some diminution of the initial penal response. The respected process, on account of which the discount is also granted, is that by which a person can attend the disapprobation visited upon him by his initial punishment and can alter his course of conduct accordingly. In viewing the person as a moral agent, we initially assume him capable of such a response and thus give him his 'second chance'.

Why, however, give up the discount after a certain number of repetitions? It is because repetitions can less and less plausibly be characterised as a lapse—a temporary failure of moral inhibition. Repetition after confrontation with penal censure also suggests a failure on the part of the offender to make the effort at self-restraint which should be the response to having been confronted with censure.

Might there be special instances where we would be reluctant to treat continued offending as a failure to take the previous condemnation seriously? Arguably, there might, where the continued offending is linked with other special indicia of reduced culpability. An example of such reduced culpability would be that of the repeat offender of limited intelligence, whose continued offending may be attributable to an inability to fully understand the censure that the previous conviction conveys.[10]

---

[10] Under Swedish law, such an offender could claim mitigation, on grounds that the conduct was based on 'a manifest lack of development, experience, or capacity for judgment'. Swedish Criminal Code, Ch 29, s 3.

Adopting this 'tolerance thesis' does not involve adopting the career-desert perspective against which I argued earlier in this chapter—for my argument presupposes that the person is being judged primarily for his present conduct. Career-desert judgements would be different: the seriousness of the present crime would be only a factor to be considered in the sentence, along with the extent and seriousness of the previous offences; if those prior crimes were serious enough, an offender convicted of a lesser offence might now receive a substantial punishment.

Have I just reinvented rehabilitation? Giving offenders a 'second chance' might sound like a rehabilitative claim, but it is not. I do not assert that the discount for first offending will in fact induce future compliance by the actor more effectively than a full dose of punishment would. The first-offender discount reflects, instead, an ethical judgement concerning tolerance for human fallibility, and concerning moral agents' capacity for attending to the censure in punishment.

What has been so troublesome about traditional penal rehabilitationism is that punishment is not made to depend on the blameworthiness of the offender's criminal choices, but rather on his supposed future amenability to treatment. According to this rehabilitationist view, the availability of any discount would depend on how responsive the offender is expected to be to his sentence. If he is deemed the 'amenable' type (who could learn better self-control from a scaled-down first dose of punishment, plus whatever treatment programmes seem to be indicated) he would be punished less. But if he is considered the 'unamenable' type, the discount would be denied. On my suggested account, however, no such picking and choosing would be permissible. The discount should be available to *every* offender until he has accumulated the requisite number of prior convictions to lose it; it does not depend on the particular offender's expected degree of responsiveness to treatment. The reason for this is, again, suggested by the communicative view of desert advocated in this volume: every offender, as a human being, is deemed a moral agent capable of understanding the censure expressed through punishment and responding accordingly. The person gradually forfeits the tolerance, and loses the associated penal discount, only through his actual subsequent criminal choices.

While this account thus is not a reinvention of the rehabilitative sentence, it embodies something we instinctively feel is legitimate behind the idea of rehabilitation. This is not the conventional positivist idea that sentences should be based on offenders' diagnosed treatability. It is, rather, that people's capacity to take condemnation of their acts seriously is something that has a moral dimension and should be acknowledged in the criminal law.

7.4 MULTIPLE PREVIOUS OFFENDING?

How many repetitions must occur before the discount should disappear? It should be clear that the progressive-loss-of-mitigation discount would not permit deductions to be made indefinitely. If the offender keeps on returning to crime, he should lose the discount entirely, and must face the full measure of punishment for his latest offence.

Among those who do respond and cease offending, there appear to be (at least) two prototypes. One is that of the conventionally behaved individual who errs in an uncharacteristic moment of impulsiveness or unwisdom, and then having been punished corrects his behaviour. Here, giving him a single 'second chance' might well suffice.

Another kind of response is one familiar to criminologists studying desistance among convicted criminals. It is that of the offender who embarks on a criminal career, but then—after having been apprehended and punished on several occasions—begins to make efforts to desist. The efforts may be halting at first: while he appears to have developed a bona fide desire to stop, he fails initially to implement it well and backslides from time to time. Eventually, however, he does come to cease offending. The pattern is that of a halting, gradual desistance that tends to be linked with the offender's age, his apparent desire to assume a more conventional lifestyle, and his dissatisfaction with the hazard of a criminal existence.[11] The progressive-loss-of-mitigation model serves to address this second kind of situation. Because the discount is withdrawn gradually, it provides a continuing moral inducement for change on the offender's part in his mode of living.

---

[11] For empirical evidence on varying patterns of desistance among convicted offenders, see JH Laub and RJ Sampson, 'Understanding Desistance from Crime' in M Tonry (ed), *Crime and Justice: A Review of Research* (Chicago, Chicago University Press, 2001) Vol 28; Alex R Piquero, DP Farrington and A Blumstein (2003) 'The Criminal Career Paradigm' in M Tonry (ed), *Crime and Justice: A Review of Research* (Chicago, Chicago University Press, 2003) Vol 30, 359.

My previous discussions of this issue of prior offending did not draw sufficient attention to the distinction between these cases. My efforts to provide a rationale for the discount model thus reverted to language which was more suitable to the first kind of case than the second. I spoke of the offender as having had a previous pattern of compliance, and of having offended in a moment of weakness or wilfulness. This mode of discourse makes sense for everyday contexts, where we are chiefly speaking of misconduct among conventionally behaved individuals. A modified vocabulary and way of thinking is needed, however, when speaking of gradual desistance among convicted criminals.

Why this distinction between the criminal law and other, everyday settings? A reason concerns whether there are selective entry criteria. One can insist on narrower allowances for previous acts of misconduct, when (as in appointing someone to an academic or judicial post) one can select only the more promising candidates, and deal with repeat offending through the eventual exclusion of the person from the activity. Criminal sentencing should operate with more generous tolerances for repeated offending, because it cannot have the luxuries of restrictive entry criteria, and exclusion for persistent violators.

7.5 THE INSTITUTIONAL AND SOCIAL CONTEXT

The foregoing point about selective entry criteria can be seen as part of a more general one: that the generosity or stringency of norms concerning repeated wrongdoing should depend, significantly, on the institutional and legal context. The criminal law should adopt generous standards concerning repeated wrongdoing, in virtue of the type of enterprise it involves. Other types of activity might well adopt more rigorous requirements for their disciplinary standards. Of particular relevance here would be: (i) the degree of stringency suitable for the system's behavioural norms; (ii) the degree of voluntariness of participation in the enterprise in question, and the ease of exit from it; and (iii) the potential severity of sanctions for violations. On these dimensions, the criminal law differs in important respects from many other forms of activity—and these differences should affect how multiple wrongdoing should be treated. We thus should pay heed to the institutional context of prior-criminal-record judgements, and to the criminal law's particular role and function.

Consider, first, a non-criminal form of regulation: a university's disciplinary procedures. Given the importance accorded to original scholarship for a university's academic work, a case can be made for stringent standards concerning (say) plagiarism. Perhaps, a modest severity-discount might be allowed for lesser first instances of this kind of misconduct. But repetition of the behaviour (and arguably also, more serious first-time offending) should result in expulsion of the offending faculty member. Thus, not much scope for 'lapses' should be allowed. Why not? The three factors just mentioned may help to provide an explanation. Thus, (i) a university should hold its academic members to high standards of scholarship and scholarly ethics; (ii) participation in the university's academic enterprise is voluntary. Those who are not willing or able to abide by these norms of scholarship, and so risk disciplinary action by the university, would be free to choose some other, less demanding occupation; (iii) the sanctions the university can levy are of a restricted nature: no loss of liberty, or deprivation of civil rights, may be imposed as a sanction. Even the ultimate academic penalty—expulsion—would leave the individual free to pursue other employment.

The criminal law should operate with less stringent norms concerning previous misconduct because the character of enterprise is different, especially in the three respects just mentioned. Thus (1) the criminal law's standards of appropriate behaviour should be less demanding—because those standards should serve to establish the minimum norms of social interaction among citizens. (2) The duty to abide by the criminal law's norms of conduct is not voluntary. Everyone must comply. No person who dislikes obeying the penal law's behavioural standards may quit the enterprise (as the plagiarising academic can), short of emigration or suicide. (3) The criminal law's sanctions are especially burdensome, and include deprivation of liberty. These three factors should call for less stringent norms in criminal law, including those relating to repetitive misconduct.

Another aspect of dealing with criminal recidivism is worth noting, and militates in favour of having a diminishing discount over several repetitions. Criminal activity tends to diminish with age, and only a minority of offenders remain involved in criminal activity for protracted periods.[12] The progressive-loss-of-mitigation approach would give offenders greater opportunity to respond to penal censure and its moral appeal, before being confronted with the full measure of the penalty. By that time, the offender's propensity for offending might well be diminishing, in any event.

7.6 AN ILLUSTRATION: SWEDEN'S TREATMENT OF REOFFENDING

How might such a progressive-loss-of-mitigation model work in practice? Sweden's scheme for sentencing recidivists provides an illustration. Under that country's sentencing law, the principle of proportionality is the governing principle, so that the seriousness of the defendant's offence is the primary determinant of penalty severity. Generally, Sweden's statute gives only limited weight to previous convictions: defendants convicted of serious crimes receive custodial sentences, even if not convicted before; and lesser offenders are given non-custodial sanctions even after repeated reoffending.

In the middle range of crime-seriousness (eg for burglaries), however, the criminal record plays a significant role—but one that comports with the 'discount' approach suggested here. Upon the first and several subsequent convictions, the offender is not imprisoned, but instead receives a non-custodial sanction. Imprisonment is imposed only as a last resort, after the offender has accumulated a significant number of convictions—perhaps as many as four or so. Until that point is reached, there would be a gradation in the degree of onerousness of the non-custodial responses, depending on the number of earlier convictions. A first offender could receive as his discounted penalty a unit fine—ie a monetary equivalent to a specified number of days' earnings, with that number depending on the seriousness of his offence. A subsequent conviction would attract a somewhat higher unit fine or possibly a term of probation involving intensive supervision in

---

[12] Laub and Sampson 2001; A von Hirsch and L Kazemian, 'Predictive Sentencing and Selective Incapacitation' in A von Hirsch, A Ashworth and JV Roberts (eds), *Principled Sentencing: Readings in Theory and Policy* (Oxford, Hart Publishing, 2009) Ch 3.

the community. For further reoffending, there would be an additional adjustment, eg a stint of community service as a penalty. It is only when the person persists in offending that he would face the full deserved sanction of a prison term.

This illustration from Sweden suggests how a progressive-loss-of-mitigation model might work in practice. It also suggests the desert model's further attraction, of helping to limit reliance on severe penal interventions. A Swedish burglar would continue receiving non-custodial sanctions, over several reconvictions—albeit ones of increasing oner-ousness. It is only with frequent reoffending—say, on the third or fourth conviction—that he would suffer the full penalty of a term of imprisonment (albeit still one of comparatively modest duration). The scheme thus helps incorporate a degree of 'parsimony' into the norms of deserved punishment.

My espousal of Sweden's approach, however, is normative and desert-oriented; I am not suggesting that adopting such a gradually diminishing discount would promote desistance better and thus reduce crime. Crime rates generally show little responsiveness to changes in sentencing patterns.[13] Adopting a discount, and making it a gradually diminishing one over several repetitions, is thus unlikely to have much impact on rates of offending.

I am also not suggesting that Sweden's norm—of a gradually dimin-ishing discount through several repetitions—'tracks' actual desistance patterns. Among offenders who do cease offending, desistance pat-terns will vary. Some will stop committing crimes after the second or third offence—and get the benefit of a portion of the discount. Others will pursue lengthy criminal careers before even beginning to make significant efforts to desist. The latter individuals would not be eligible for a discount, because their desistance would occur too late. Sweden's rule on repeat offending should be thus seen as normatively based. Its criteria thus should reflect on what appears reasonable as implementation of the progressive-loss-of-mitigation principles, taking into account institutional and social context within which the criminal sanction operates.

---

[13] Bottoms and von Hirsch 2010, 107–13.

7.7 SERIOUSNESS AND NUMBER OF PREVIOUS CONVICTIONS

To what extent should the seriousness of the previous convictions count? In everyday judgements of censure, the gravity of the prior misconduct would make a difference. Suppose someone has committed a serious intentional wrong, and wants to claim that his act is uncharacteristic of his past behaviour. Suppose he has previously been censured for other misdeeds—but ones of much less serious character. He might still plausibly argue that it was uncharacteristic of him to commit serious wrongs; he might claim, 'Yes, I've committed petty acts of misconduct before, but this is the first time I've done something *this* bad.'

Similar logic should hold for sentencing. Someone convicted of his first serious crime should be entitled to plead that such gravely reprehensible conduct has been uncharacteristic of him, and hence that he deserves to have his penalty scaled down—even where he has a record of lesser infractions. Where the current offence is serious, in other words, the adjustment for the criminal history should take into account the gravity of prior convictions as well as their frequency.[14]

How many repetitions may occur before the 'tolerance' plea loses its force entirely? I have no ready answer, as this seems a matter of judgement. I have suggested here that the discount should be lost entirely after several convictions, but there is no magic number. But it should be apparent from what has already been said that after several repetitions, the plea will have been spent, and the offender should get the 'full measure' of punishment appropriate for a crime of that degree of gravity. If, after that, the actor commits further repetitions, he should get no severer response: there simply would be no mitigation due, and the person would be punished as before. Were it permissible to keep on increasing the punitive response with each subsequent repetition, even relatively routine misconduct could eventually receive unduly severe penalties.

---

[14] See von Hirsch 1981, 615–16, 620–21. Suppose, however, that the current crime is not serious. Then, it becomes more debatable to what extent the gravity of prior offences should count. When someone has been convicted of a minor property crime, for example, it should not seem to matter whether such prior offences were other such lesser offences, or offences of a more serious character such as burglary or robbery. In any event, the offender's record shows that crimes of at least the present degree of seriousness are not uncharacteristic of him.

The present topic, concerning the role of the defendant's previous criminal convictions in sentencing, is one on which a divergence of opinion exists among desert theorists. Besides my own perspective, described here, two other analyses have recently been put forward— one by the Oxford criminologist Julian Roberts, and the other by the American legal scholar Youngjae Lee. Roberts contends that progressive loss of mitigation may be accounted for by conceptions of an offender's culpability;[15] Lee invokes a theory of criminal omissions instead.[16]

For further reading:

Bagaric, Mirko (2014) 'The Punishment Should Fit the Crime—Not the Prior Convictions of the Person that Committed the Crime' (2014) *San Diego Law Review* 51, 343.

Lee, Youngjae (2010) 'Repeat Offenders and the Question of Desert' in JV Roberts and A von Hirsch (eds), *Previous Convictions at Sentencing* (Oxford, Hart Publishing) Ch 4.

Roberts, Julian V (2010) 'First Offender Discounts: Exploring the Justifications' in JV Roberts and A von Hirsch (eds), *Previous Convictions at Sentencing: Theoretical and Applied Perspectives* (Oxford, Hart Publishing) Ch 2.

von Hirsch, Andrew (2010) 'Proportionality and Progressive Loss of Mitigation: Some Further Reflections' in A von Hirsch and JV Roberts (eds), *Previous Convictions at Sentencing: Theoretical and Applied Perspectives* (Oxford, Hart Publishing) Ch 1.

---

[15] JV Roberts, 'First Offender Sentencing Discounts: Exploring the Justifications' in JV Roberts and A von Hirsch (eds), *Previous Convictions at Sentencing* (Oxford, Hart Publishing, 2010) Ch 2.

[16] Y Lee, 'Repeat Offenders and the Question of Desert' in Roberts and von Hirsch 2010, Ch 4. The omission, according to this author, consists in the defendant's failure to alter his lifestyle after his first conviction, so as to make offending less tempting.

8

Proportionate Non-custodial Sanctions

IMPRISONMENT—AND ESPECIALLY, IMPRISONMENT for significant durations—is a severe penalty. Under a proportionality-oriented sentencing scheme, the sanction should thus be reserved for crimes of a serious nature. Other, less serious offences should be dealt through non-custodial sanctions that are less onerous than imprisonment. A properly constructed penalty system therefore requires norms and principles guiding the scaling and use of such non-custodial sanctions.

How might non-custodial sanctions be arrayed, under a desert rationale? The English legal scholar Martin Wasik and I have proposed a model.[1] In this chapter, I shall describe the Wasik–von Hirsch scheme and address the issues it raises: those concerning scaling of non-custodial sanctions, comparability among penalties, and back-up sanctions for breach.

8.1 BASIC ELEMENTS OF THE MODEL

The Wasik–von Hirsch model embodies the following elements:

— Non-custodial sanctions are to be graded in severity according to the seriousness of the offender's crimes. 'Intermediate'

---

[1] M Wasik and A von Hirsch (1988), 'Non-Custodial Penalties and the Principles of Desert' (1988) *Criminal Law Review* 555. That article made use of numerical sentencing tariffs for heuristic purposes, in order to make explicit the relationships between the various elements of the scheme system. However, a desert model does not presuppose the actual establishment of such numerical standards—since other techniques of guidance, such as Swedish-style statutory guiding principles, or English-style narrative guidelines, may be a preferable way of assisting judges in making sentencing choices (on this issue of numerical guidelines versus statutory sentencing principles; see A von Hirsch, 'Sentencing by Numbers or Words?' in M Wasik and K Pease (eds), *Sentencing Reform: Guidance or Guidelines?* (Manchester,

sanctions—that is, non-custodial sanctions of the middle range of severity—should thus be employed only for crimes of medium seriousness, and not for lesser crimes.

— Substitution would be permitted among sanctions of comparable degrees of onerousness, but with policy-based limitations (discussed below) on how extensive that substitution may be.

— There would be significant restrictions on the severity of the back-up sanctions that may be used against offenders who violate the conditions of a non-custodial sentence.

Such a scheme has a number of advantages. First, it is capable of restricting the use of imprisonment. Imprisonment, as a severe sanction, would be reserved for crimes of higher ranges of gravity. Offences of intermediate and lesser seriousness should generally draw noncustodial penalties.

Second, the scheme would restrict the use of intermediate sanctions (for example, non-custodial sanctions that deprive offenders of significant portions of their income or leisure time) to crimes that are of middle-level gravity. Such sanctions should not be used for low-level offences, merely because their perpetrators are deemed potentially more co-operative with programme requirements. It is the defendant who commits (say) a substantial theft, not the petty thief, who should be a candidate for such sanctions.

The scale of punishments could be kept reasonably simple, because of the limits on interchangeability described below. For each level of sanction severity, one type of penalty would ordinarily be prescribed. Substitutions of penalties of equivalent onerousness would be permitted, but only when there were special reasons—for example, the defendant's inability to perform the tasks of the normally-recommended punishment. Free substitution would be barred, as would be the piling up of multiple non-custodial sanctions on individual defendants.

Finally, the revocation sanction would be brought under control. Offenders should not have to suffer lengthy stints of imprisonment, merely because they had breached the technical conditions of a non-custodial sentence.

Manchester University Press, 1987); A von Hirsch, K Knapp and M Tonry, *The Sentencing Commission and its Guidelines* (Boston, Northeastern University Press, 1987) Ch 3. For further discussion, see S Rex, *Reforming Community Penalties* (London, Routledge, 2013) .

Each of these various features merits closer examination. Let me begin with the question of substitution among penalties.

8.2 INTERCHANGES: EQUIVALENT PENAL BITE

In fashioning guidelines for use of imprisonment, the question of substitutability among sanctions seldom arises, because imprisonment (especially for substantial periods) is so much more severe than other penalties. With non-custodial sanctions, however, the problem presents itself in earnest: several penalties of comparable onerousness may exist, and it is necessary to decide which should be invoked when deciding sentence.

The criterion for substitutions among penalties should, on a desert model, be that of comparable severity: approximate equivalence in penal bite. The principle of proportionality addresses the *severity* of penalties, not their particular form. When sanctions are ordered according to the gravity of crimes, replacing one kind of penalty by another of having roughly the same degree of onerousness does not disturb ordinal proportionality: that is, it disturbs neither the parity nor the rank-ordering of penal responses (see Chapter 5).

Employing the foregoing criterion, of approximate equivalence in severity, requires assessing the comparative onerousness of the various penalties involved: is a fine of how many weeks' earnings, for example, 'worth' one week under probation supervision? Severity, I have suggested previously (Chapter 6), is a matter of how much a sanction intrudes upon the interests a person typically needs to live an adequate existence. Gauging comparative severity thus would involve assessing how much the various sanctions typically would intrude on a person's standard of living.

What of crime-prevention concerns? A desert rationale does not permit crime prevention aims to be relied upon to decide among penalties of substantially differing severity, as that would infringe ordinal proportionality requirements (particularly, the requirement of parity).[2] That is the objection to schemes such as selective incapacitation, wherein prison terms of markedly different lengths are to be imposed on offenders convicted of comparably serious crimes, depending on

---

[2] For discussion of the parity requirements of proportionality, see ch 5.

those persons' predicted likelihood of returning to crime. When two types of penalties have approximately the same penal bite, however, the parity-requirement of proportionality[3] is satisfied—in which event one penalty may be chosen over the other on crime prevention grounds.

Professor AE Bottoms provides an illustration.[4] Suppose two offenders, *A* and *B*, are convicted for comparable offences of intermediate seriousness. *A* has no previous convictions, and has a fairly 'stable' social background. The other offender, *B*, has a substantial criminal record. Since the desert model allows the lack of prior convictions to be treated as extenuating to a limited extent (see Chapter 7), *A* deserves a somewhat reduced penalty compared to *B*. The criminal record, however, is also an indicator of risk, and how should that be taken into account? The offender's likelihood of returning to crime should not, under a desert model, justify any large severity-differential. However, risk may be used to decide the form of the penalty: Thus *A* might receive a conditional sentence with a financial penalty, whereas *B*'s sanction might involve a period of intensive probation supervision, aimed at reducing (at least partially) his likelihood of reoffending. Provided these penalties have the approximately adjusted penal bite, the requirements of ordinal proportionality would be satisfied.

Numerical sentencing guidelines, such as Minnesota's, tend to have a firm demarcation between custodial and non-custodial sanctions. The sentencing tariff prescribes various periods of custody for conduct above a certain level of seriousness, and non-custodial sanctions for lesser conduct.[5] Any such 'hard' demarcation has its drawbacks, however: it can, for example, mean unduly sharp transitions in severity as one moves up the penalty scale from non-custodial measures to custody.

---

[3] See at ch 5, section 5.2 above.

[4] AE Bottoms, 'The Concept of Intermediate Sanctions and its Relevance for the Probation Service' in E Shaw and K Haines (eds), *The Criminal Justice System: A Central Role for the Probation Service* (Cambridge, Institute of Criminology, 1989).

[5] For a more extensive analysis of Minnesota's and Oregon's numerical sentencing guidelines, see A von Hirsch, 'Proportionality and Parsimony in American Sentencing Guidelines: the Minnesota and Oregon Standards' in CMV Clarkson and R Morgan (eds), *The Politics of Sentencing Reform* (Oxford, Oxford University Press, 1995) Ch 6, and RS Frase, *Just Sentencing: Principles and Procedures for a Workable System* (New York, Oxford University Press, 2013) Ch 3. For numerical guidelines generally, see ch 1, discussion at nn 30–33.

A desert rationale requires no such sharp demarcation, because limited periods of incarceration may be equivalent in severity to more onerous non-custodial sanctions.[6] When this equivalence exists, substitutions should be permissible. The penalty-scale thus might, in its high ranges, prescribe substantial periods of incarceration, without permitted substitution. The next lower bands of penalties might provide for rather intrusive community sanctions, such as home detention (with electronic monitoring). Here, however, short periods of full custody— measured in days or weeks—could be permitted as a substitute. The substitute might be invoked, for example, for offenders whose previous records of absconding suggest they would not be likely to comply with a home-detention order. The duration of that full custody would have to be modest, however; and would be calibrated so as to compare in its severity to the normally applicable non-custodial sentence. Any such authority to interchange short prison terms with other sanctions, it is to be emphasised, should be limited to crimes in the upper-middle range of seriousness. If imprisonment became a permissible option for crimes of lesser seriousness, the entire policy of proportionate, non-custodial sanctions would be compromised.

Should there be any policy-based limits on substitutability? A desert rationale might allow varying degrees of substitutability—from none to a wide degree. At one extreme there would be a penalty scale with no substitutions permitted. That penalty scale would consist of bands of penalties of ascending onerousness, with (say) cautions and small fines at the bottom of the scale, more significant financial penalties next, community service thereafter, and full custody at the top. Within each band, a single type of sanction could be prescribed: for crimes in the intermediate range of gravity, for example, substantial monetary penalties (relative to income) might be the only sanction prescribed. Such a scheme would grade conduct according to the seriousness of the offence, as proportionality requires. It could also significantly reduce the use of imprisonment, by requiring that custody would be restricted to crimes in the higher ranges of seriousness. Nevertheless, its rigidity would be a significant drawback. It would, for example, bar the courts from substituting probation for a normally-applicable financial penalty,

---

[6] See, however, N Padfield, 'Time to Bury the Custody "Threshold"?' (2011) *Criminal Law Review* 8, 593.

even for offenders who might be responsive to such supervision. The prescribed sanction in a given band, moreover, may not be capable of being carried out for certain types of offenders. Financial penalties for crimes in the lower-intermediate range, for example, could not be collected from offenders lacking in regular earnings.

At the opposite pole could be a 'full-substitution' scheme. Any given penalty could be substituted for any other, provided that the resulting severity is not altered. There could be numerical sentencing standards which prescribe, not particular sanctions, but 'sanction units' instead— that is, units of severity. A crime of upper-intermediate gravity, for example, would be punishable by a prescribed number of sanction units. These sanction units then would be translatable into actual penalties, depending on the latter's severity. The appropriate penalty-unit sentence could, then, be carried out through a variety of sentencing options. Different penalties could also be combined, so as to achieve the prescribed total number of units.

This latter approach, however, has significant practical drawbacks. It presupposes a degree of sophistication in the ability to calibrate and compare the onerousness of different sanctions that is not likely to exist. In a scheme with limited substitutions, we can make a judgement about whether the prescribed sanctions are arrayed approximately in the order of their severity. The more numerous and easily combined the sanctions are, however, the more elusive the task of comparing penalties becomes. Moreover, it is not clear why full substitutability is needed. There are two main kinds of situations where substitutions would be useful: (1) where the normally-applicable sanctions cannot feasibly be enforced and a more easily enforceable substitute is called for, and (2) where a substitute might possibly have an enhanced preventive effect, as in AE Bottoms' previously-cited example.[7] There might conceivably be some other occasions for substitution as well, but it is not obvious what useful purpose would be served by cafeteria-style sentencing with unrestricted substitutions.

What remains is *limited* substitutability, with some sanctions preferred over others of equivalent severity—and this is what the Wasik–von Hirsch model envisions. According to that approach, one type of punishment would be prescribed on the scale for each level of sanction

---

[7] See text at n 3 above.

severity, which would be the normally-recommended disposition. However, the substitution of other types of sanctions of comparable severity could be invoked for certain specified reasons. Those reasons might be preventive (where, for example, the sentencer had special reasons for believing that the alternative sanction could help induce the offender to refrain from reoffending), or administrative (where, for example, the standard sentence could not effectively be enforced against this type of defendant). Sweden opts for this approach of limited substitutability—for example, it permits intensive probation to be substituted for conditional-sentence-plus-fine, for offenders who are believed to be potentially responsive to probation supervision.[8]

8.3 BACK-UP SANCTIONS FOR BREACH OF CONDITIONS

Non-custodial sanctions require back-up sanctions. Something needs to be done with the individual who, say, is placed on probation but refuses to comply with the supervision-routines he is required to observe.

In Anglo-American jurisdictions, the breach sanction has tended to be imprisonment. The form of traditional, non-custodial sanctions made that apparent. Probation, for example, consists of a conditional disposition whereby a sentence of imprisonment is suspended, provided that the offender abides by specified conditions of supervision in the community. If the offender violates those conditions, the prison sentence held in reserve may be invoked.

Relying on incarceration extensively as the breach sanction is troublesome, however, especially for intermediate sanctions. Offenders receiving these sanctions often have extensive requirements to fulfil, and their compliance tends to be more thoroughly monitored. Violations are thus more likely to be uncovered than would be the case for traditional non-custodial sanctions, such as fines or probation.[9] Easy resort to imprisonment for breaching the conditions of a non-custodial sentence, however, would mean that many more such offenders could end up in prison.

---

[8] Swedish Penal Code Ch 30, s 7.
[9] In many (especially American) jurisdictions, probation has been routinely resorted to as the non-custodial penalty of choice, with large caseloads and minimal actual supervision.

When someone fails or refuses to observe the required routines of a non-custodial sanction, the breach can be seen as involving two components. (1) The offender has not yet completed his original sentence, and still 'owes' that uncompleted portion in some comparable form. (2) The act of breach is, arguably, itself a reprehensible act, calling for some added penalty. With these elements identified, it is evident why a desert rationale should restrict the severity of breach sanctions; thus:

— Element (1) would call for the uncompleted portion of the original penalty to be served in some different, more easily-enforced form. It does not, by definition, justify a more severe response.

— Element (2) would call for a modest addition in penal bite, depending how reprehensible the act of breach itself is deemed to be. The question is, how reprehensible? Victimising acts can be gauged in their gravity by the extent to which they typically intrude upon a victim's quality of life (see Chapter 6, section 6.1), but the act of breach *per se* lacks a victim. No theoretical framework has yet been developed for judging the reprehensibility of such conduct. Intuitively, however, breach seems hardly comparable with acts (say, those of violence) that would be deemed serious enough for resorting to imprisonment—especially for longer periods.

On the basis of such arguments, the Wasik–von Hirsch model envisions, in case of breach, only a modest step-up in severity. A breach might result in the offender receiving a sanction that is one band in severity up from the band in which his initial penalty was located.[10] Whether this particular rule should be adopted depends on the character of the penalty structure—and also on a judgement concerning the degree of blameworthiness of element (2)—the act of breach. The principle, however, should be apparent: breach should call only for a modest penalty increase, and imprisonment should be sparingly invoked as the breach sanction.

Thus far, we have been speaking of breaches of those conditions of a non-custodial penalty which prescribe the nature of the routines

---

[10] For heuristic purposes, the Wasik and von Hirsch's model sets forth a series of bands of ascending sentence severity, depending on the seriousness-range of the offence. This solution permits moving one band upward as the breach penalty. See A von Hirsch, Andrew and A Ashworth, *Proportionate Sentencing: Exploring the Principles* (Oxford, Oxford University Press, 2005) Ch 9, 155–61.

which the offender must undergo as his punishment. Some kinds of non-custodial sanctions—probation for example—impose the additional condition that the offender refrain from committing further crimes. Reoffending, however, should be treated differently: as a situation of recidivism. The sentence should thus depend primarily on the degree of seriousness of the new criminal act—with the modest adjustment for repetition that was suggested in the previous chapter on previous convictions (Chapter 7). Imprisonment would thus be warranted only if the behaviour would—taking this adjustment into account—be deemed serious enough to justify a custodial sentence.

For further reading:

Bottoms, AE, S Rex and G Robinson (eds) (2013) *Alternatives to Prison* (London, Routledge).

Kahan, Dan M (1996) 'What Do Alternative Sanctions Mean?' *University of Chicago Law Review* 63, 591.

Lovegrove, Austin (2001) 'Sanctions and Severity: To the Demise of von Hirsch & Wasik's Sanction Hierarchy' *Howard Journal of Criminal Justice* 40, 126.

Morris, Norval and M Tonry (1991) *Between Prison and Probation: Intermediate Punishments in a Rational Sentencing System* (New York, Oxford University Press).

Padfield, N (2011) 'Time to Bury the Custody "Threshold"?' *Criminal Law Review* 8, 593.

9

A 'Modified' Desert Model?

DESERT THEORY SETS priorities among sentencing aims: it holds that it is more important to have proportionately-ordered sanctions than to seek ulterior objectives—such as incapacitating those who are deemed likely to return to crime. This understandably evokes discomfort: why can't we seek proportionality *and* pursue other desired ends, whether they be treatment, incapacitation or deterrence?

To a considerable degree, a desert model does permit consideration of other aims: namely, where that would be consistent with the proportionate ordering of penalties. Thus when there is a choice between two non-custodial sanctions of approximately equivalent severity, proportionality constraints are not offended when one of these is chosen over the other on, say, rehabilitative grounds. Desert theorists have thus come forward with schemes designed to incorporate such other aims. The sanctions would be ranked in severity according to the gravity of the crime, but alternative penalties of roughly equivalent onerousness could be substituted when, say, rehabilitative concerns so indicate (see Chapter 8, section 8.2). Nevertheless, a desert model remains significantly constraining: such ulterior aims may be relied upon only where this would not substantially alter the comparative onerousness of the penalties. Why not, then, adopt a 'mixed' model, that relaxes the proportionality constraints to a degree, in order to allow increased scope for pursuing other penal aims?

I shall be speaking here about mixed models of a certain sort: namely, those that permit only a limited degree of derogation from the principle of proportionality. If proportionality is an important fairness constraint, as argued in this volume, it should restrict the pursuit of ulterior ends, including those of crime prevention. Mixed models that depart from proportionality in specified situations and to an appropriately limited extent still may qualify as broadly equitable schemes. It is that kind of scheme that may be termed a 'modified' desert model.

The reader will detect a certain tentativeness here. It is not easy to construct a theory that allows one to determine when proportionality may be overridden in the pursuit of other goals. What makes this issue still more difficult is that the models of which I am speaking would depart from proportionality only to a limited extent. Thus on one hand, one cannot dismiss such schemes as being manifestly unfair; but on the other, it is not easy to discern how much additional benefit may be obtained from such restricted departures. The point of examining these hybrids is to make it clear that a commitment to proportionality does not rule out pursuit of other objectives: that we may agree that sanctions should be proportionate in the main, and still consider certain degrees of deviation.

9.1 EXCEPTIONAL DEPARTURES

In examining mixed schemes, it might be helpful to begin with one suggested several decades ago by the American penal theorist Paul Robinson.[1] Under his proposed model, penalties should ordinarily be scaled according to crimes' seriousness, as required by the principle of proportionality. Upward deviations from ordinal desert requirements would be permitted, however, in certain exceptional circumstances—namely, when needed to prevent 'intolerable levels of crime'. Robinson would impose a further limitation on such departures: that even when the prevention of serious criminal offending is at issue, *gross* deviations from proportionality would not be allowed. Robinson couches his formula in general terms—in terms such as preventing an 'intolerable' increase in crime rates. What is or is not tolerable is a matter of judgement, and Robinson is not so much offering a criterion as a way of thinking about departures.

How might one defend Robinson's model? A simple argument would be to invoke the analogy of quarantining persons with serious and easily communicable diseases. Quarantined persons surely do not deserve to lose their liberty, for it is generally not their fault that they are disease carriers. They are deprived of their freedom solely in order to protect the survival and health of numerous other persons. The reason

---

[1] PH Robinson, 'Hybrid Principles for the Distribution of Criminal Sanctions' (1987) *Northwestern Law Review* 82, 19.

for quarantining those with pandemic diseases is that community survival is deemed paramount to concerns about justice.

The quarantine parallel, however, is not helpful when given closer scrutiny. The criminal harm at issue here is not comparable in magnitude to the catastrophic consequences of pandemic diseases: common crimes, for example, represent no such public-safety threat as plague or cholera epidemics.

Punishment, unlike quarantine, also involves blaming. The person who receives extended punishment suffers added penal censure that is not warranted by the seriousness of his or her conduct—whereas we do not treat quarantined individuals as *deserving* of confinement. The quarantine analogy is also too ambitious. A quarantined person may be detained indefinitely, without regard to fault, as long as he remains a disease carrier. Robinson's model, however, would only ease desert constraints in exceptional situations, not eliminate them—because of his limit that the extra punishment must not itself be grossly disproportionate.

If not quarantine, what other argument can be made? Ronald Dworkin's model of rights may be helpful here.[2] Dworkin maintains that constraints of fairness constitute claims against the general welfare: a justice constraint should be respected, that is, even if disregarding it were to provide greater aggregate social benefits. An example of such a justice constraint is the requirement of proof beyond reasonable doubt in criminal trials. This is designed to prevent the unfairness of convicting innocent people, and should apply even if a lower standard-of-proof were to provide increased crime-preventive benefits by making it easier to convict actually guilty persons.[3]

Fairness claims, on Dworkin's analysis, are *prima facie* claims, however: they may sometimes be overridden when the countervailing concerns are of sufficient urgency. An overriding ground, Dworkin suggests, is when the loss of social utility involved in maintaining the fairness constraint is of extraordinary dimensions: when, in his words, 'the cost to society would not simply be incremental, but would be of a degree beyond the [social] cost paid to grant the original right, a degree

---

[2] D Dworkin, *Taking Rights Seriously* (Cambridge, Massachusetts, Harvard University Press, 1977) Ch 7.

[3] Dworkin speaks of his model of 'rights', but his analysis also applies to other fairness constraints, including those discussed in the text.

great enough to justify whatever assault on dignity or equality might be involved'.[4]

When, on this approach, might the proportionality principle have to yield to crime-prevention concerns? Not ordinarily, since the very point of treating proportionality as a fairness constraint is to restrict pursuit of other, utilitarian goals in deciding sentence—particularly, those of crime control. But even if this constraint on crime-preventive goals should hold in ordinary circumstances, it might under Dworkin's approach be required to yield when the loss of utility of crime prevention would otherwise be of unusually great dimensions. Dworkin's conception of defeasible fairness constraints, therefore, would seem to be a plausible way of supplying a rationale for modified desert schemes.

One issue under Robinson's model concerns the force of the *prima facie* fairness constraint. Some fairness constraints seem to be less readily overridden than others. Consider the requirement of proof beyond reasonable doubt: it would scarcely seem proper to permit *that* requirement to be trumped, even in order to avoid substantial losses of crime prevention. What Robinson must implicitly be asserting, therefore, is that proportionality is an important fairness constraint (important enough to require serious social consequences before it may be overridden), but not *so* crucial as the requirement of proof beyond reasonable doubt (where no such override would ever seem appropriate). Another question concerns the degree of urgency that is needed for the overriding utility claim. What potentially is at stake in sentencing policy questions is not community survival, as is the case with quarantine. Robinson appears to be suggesting that the criminality sought to be prevented through the departure from proportionality must involve both substantial frequency and a high degree of injuriousness—eg, a large increase in the incidence of seriously harmful conduct.

One is left largely with intuitions on these questions, because they involve comparisons of unlikes. One has, on one hand, a non-consequentialist, retrospectively-oriented demand of justice; and on the other, an override claim based on consequentialist considerations of prospective harm. No single intellectual currency exists into which these competing considerations can be translated and compared. Perhaps the case for Robinson's solution is simply that it makes proportionality not an absolute constraint, but an important one.

[4] Dworkin 1977, 200.

The countervailing utilities must be weighty for an override to be warranted. Moreover, the extent of permitted deviation from proportionality should also be somewhat restricted. Gross departures would be impermissible—because such manifestly disproportionate responses would wholly misrepresent the degree of the person's blameworthiness.

The Robinson hybrid has undeniable appeal. Whilst abiding by desert constraints ordinarily, it permits departures where the case for them seems the strongest. What, then, are the potential problems?

One problem concerns identifying the kind of criminal harm to be prevented. Robinson would restrict the departures from proportionality, as noted, to cases where the conduct is not only gravely harmful to its victims, but a significant frequency of that conduct is involved. This, however, would sharply restrict the scope of the exception, since there seldom exists sound empirical grounds for believing that upward departures from proportionate sentences would significantly reduce the aggregate incidence of serious criminal conduct. The desired crime-reduction effect would have to derive from general deterrence or incapacitation: either offenders are intimidated through the extra penalty or that penalty provides added net restraint on reoffending. It is, however, notoriously difficult to trace and confirm such effects (see Chapter 1).

If the requirement of traceable *aggregate* effects presents these difficulties, might it be dropped? AE Bottoms and Roger Brownsword have suggested doing so. Individuals who constitute a 'vivid danger' of seriously injuring others, these authors argue, should be given periods of extra confinement, even if such a policy were to have no measurable impact on aggregate violence levels.[5] However, those authors

---

[5] AE Bottoms and R Brownsword, 'Dangerousness and Rights' in JW Hinton (ed), *Dangerousness: Problems of Assessment and Prediction* (London, George Allen & Unwin, 1983). These authors draw on Dworkin's model of rights just discussed, for their argument. Dworkin suggests two possible grounds for overriding a right or fairness constraint. One, referred to in the text above, is where a loss of utility of extraordinary dimensions would otherwise occur. Another is where a competing right is involved, eg, when rights of free speech collide with those of privacy. In my view, it is the first of these two grounds which is relevant here: the issue is that of overriding proportionality requirements because of the extraordinary hazards to personal safety posed by certain high risk offenders. Strangely, however, Bottoms and Brownsword assert that it is the second of Dworkin's two grounds which is at issue: the offender's right to not-more-than-proportionate punishment is defeated by the potential victim's 'right' not to be injured. This I find puzzling. Granted, the victim has rights of physical safety which the offence infringes. But has the *state*

emphasise that such an exception should be invoked only when a defendant's potential criminality would involve a high likelihood of serious injury to others.

This latter standard of individual dangerousness, however, is also not easily met. To justify extension of the sentence on grounds of Bottoms and Brownsword's 'vivid danger' test, the person would need to be likely to injure others even *after* expiration of his normally-deserved term for the crime of conviction (which would be lengthy, if his crime of conviction was serious). Making such forecasts would thus require a capacity to gauge the expected duration of a criminal career that scarcely exists today.[6] The uncertainty of career durations could also mean that very long extra confinement might be needed to provide even a minimal assurance of added prevention. The longer the confinement, however, the more it collides with restraining principles, such as Robinson's, that grossly disproportionate sanctions should be avoided.

Another potential hazard is that of erosion of the standard. Essential for the Bottoms–Brownsword model is that the sentencer may impose a more-severe-than-proportionate sanction only in order to prevent very serious criminal harm. Loosening that standard, so as to admit lesser harms, compromises the basic idea: that desert constraints (as important requirements of justice) may be disregarded only in exigent circumstances. Yet how confident can one be, given the political dynamics of crime-prevention policy in many jurisdictions, that such narrowly-drawn departure standards could be sustained? May not a narrow exception be expanded too readily in the name of public protection? Someone might support such a hybrid model in theory if its tightly-drawn departure criteria were maintained, and yet still be concerned about implementing the model because of that 'if'.

---

infringed the victim's rights if it merely fails, as law enforcement so often does, to prevent injury? Suppose, particularly, that the state responds to the offender's crime by imposing a proportionate sanction. It seems implausible that this would infringe a *right* on the part of potential victims to the imposition of more severe sanctions on offenders, if this might possibly forestall future victimisation.

 [6] See AE Bottoms and A von Hirsch, 'The Crime-Preventive Impact of Penal Sanctions' in P Cane and HM Kritzer (eds), *The Oxford Handbook of Empirical Legal Studies* (Oxford, Oxford University Press, 2010) Ch 4, 114–17.

9.2 'RANGE MODELS'

Robinson's scheme, as well as Bottoms and Brownsword's, allow departures from ordinal desert only in narrowly defined situations. An alternative approach would be to allow a limited degree of relaxation of ordinal desert constraints more generally. Desert considerations could be treated as setting appropriate ranges of punishments, but within those ranges the penalty could be fixed on crime-preventive grounds. There are two different versions of such a model, having different rationales and somewhat differing practical implications. Let us consider each.

9.2a 'Limiting Retributivism'

'Limiting retributivism' is identified with the writings of Norval Morris (see Chapter 5, section 5.1). Proportionality, according to his view, should be treated as defining only certain outer limits: no more than so much punishment for a given type of offence, nor (perhaps) no less than so much. Within the resulting broad ranges, the sentence could be fixed by reference to other (chiefly crime-preventive) aims.[7] German penologists have supported a comparable view, termed the 'Spielraumtheorie'.[8]

Morris contended that his model is required by the logic of desert. Proportionality, he argued, is indeterminate: it suggests only how much punishment is *un*deserved in the sense of being manifestly excessive or lenient. Within these bounds, reliance on non-desert grounds in setting sentence is permissible because the claims of desert supposedly have been exhausted.

The deficiency of this argument has been pointed out already (Chapter 5). It overlooks the requirements of ordinal proportionality—particularly, the requirement of parity. When two defendants have been

---

[7] N Morris, *Punishment, Desert, and Rehabilitation* (Washington, DC, US Government Printing Office, 1976); N Morris, *Madness and the Criminal Law* (Chicago, Chicago University Press, 1982) Ch 8.

[8] HJ Bruns, *Das Recht der Strafzumessung*, 2nd edn (Cologne, Carl Heymanns Verlag, 1985) 105–09; F Streng, *Strafrechtliche Sanktionen: Die Strafzumessung und ihre Grundlagen*, 3rd edn (Stuttgart, Kohlhammer, 2012) 626–632.

convicted of (say) comparable serious robberies, giving one a substantially larger sentence than the other for the sake of crime prevention, visits greater disapprobation on him for conduct that is *ex hypothesi* equally reprehensible. To assert that desert, by its very logical structure, imposes only broad limits, ignores this demand for parity.

9.2b A 'Modified' Desert Model

There is, however, another way of conceptualising a 'range' model: one that would make it explicitly a modified desert theory. On this approach, the parity requirements of ordinal proportionality (see Chapter 5, section 5.2) would be relaxed to some degree. Proportionality would still determine comparative punishment rankings, but deviations would be permitted—albeit to a limited extent—in the severity of sanctions imposed on crimes of comparable seriousness. While such departures from parity requirements involve a sacrifice of equity, the extent of that sacrifice depends on how much deviation would be involved. Restricted deviations, arguably, would permit the pursuit of crime prevention objectives without 'too much' disproportionality.

This latter model differs, however, from Norval Morris's 'limiting retributivism' in that it requires closer scrutiny of inequalities in punishment. Since parity continues to be regarded as an important requirement of fairness, it matters how much deviation from parity is involved, and for how strong the ulterior reasons are. Only modest deviations, to achieve pressing ulterior objectives, would be permissible.

Under such a model, two major questions arise. The first concerns defining the limits: how much deviation from parity is to be permitted? The second is identifying the ulterior ends: for what goal (crime prevention or otherwise) may such deviations be warranted? Let us consider each of these issues, in turn.

Specifying the limits. One objection to 'limiting retributivism' has been the difficulty of delineating the applicable desert limits. On this alternative 'range' model, however, the fixing of limits becomes conceptually easier. A specified degree of deviation from ordinal desert-constraints is set as the applicable limit. Since the governing idea is that there should be only modest derogations of ordinal desert, those limits should be reasonably constrained. Perhaps a 10 or 15 per cent deviation might be permissible, but certainly not a 25 or 30 per cent one. The gravity of the criminal conduct would thus continue to substantially shape (albeit no longer fully to determine) the onerousness of punishment severity.[9] *Identifying the ulterior ends.* For what purpose should such deviations from ordinal desert be allowed? A possible purpose could be that of crime prevention: reliance on offender risk could, for example, become permissible, provided the applicable limits on deviation from ordinal desert were not exceeded. Such a strategy encounters, however, a fairness-effectiveness dilemma. A substantial incapacitative effect, for example, tends to be achievable only when the sentence differential between lower- and high-risk individuals is large.[10] Large differentials, however, would mean infringing ordinal desert constraints to a great extent—and not the limited degree which this hybrid scheme would seem to contemplate. Keeping the differentials modest, on the other hand, would restrict the preventive benefits. That, in turn, raises a further difficulty: if ordinal proportionality is a demand of fairness, even limited deviations become justifiable only by a showing of strong countervailing reasons. How could this requirement be satisfied by only modest increases in preventive effectiveness?

What other reasons might there be for deviating from desert constraints? One might be to facilitate the scaling of non-custodial penalties. Under a desert model, substitution among such sanctions would be permitted only when the penalties are equally onerous (see more fully, Chapter 8). Relaxing proportionality constraints would allow substitutions to be made somewhat more easily, and might also facilitate devising back-up sanctions for offenders who violate the terms of their sentence. This might be accomplished, moreover, while permitting only limited deviations from parity.

Where does this leave us? The attraction of the hybrids discussed here lies in that they would seem to promote other goals at only limited sacrifices of equity. Why not deviate from proportionality to

[9] For a thoughtful formulation of this perspective, see RS Frase, *Just Sentencing: Principles and Procedures for a Workable System* (New York, Oxford University Press, 2013).

[10] A von Hirsch, A Ashworth and JV Roberts (eds), *Principled Sentencing: Readings in Theory and Policy*, 3rd edn (Oxford, Hart Publishing, 2009) 98–99; See also M Haist, 'Deterrence in a Sea of Just Deserts: Are Utilitarian Goals Achievable in a World of Limiting Retributivism?' (2009) *Journal of Criminal Law & Criminology* 99, 789; M Marcus, 'Limiting Retributivism: Revisions to Model Penal Code Sentencing Provisions' (2007) *Whittier Law Review* 29, 295.

only a limited extent, or only in restricted situations, if doing so would generate added crime-prevention benefits? The achievement of these ulterior goals, however, tends to be elusive. When scenarios in which these hybrids might be employed are examined carefully, it is seldom easy to gauge how much extra prevention can really be accomplished. An emphasis on these other goals, moreover, can too easily lead to breaching the rather imprecise limits of these hybrid models. If prevention remains an important aim and restricted deviations from parity do not suffice to promote it, why not larger deviations? Large deviations, however, would mean a system that is no longer even approximately equitable. Appealing as these hybrids may seem, one needs to be cautious about the details.

For further reading:

Frase, Richard S (2013) *Just Sentencing: Principles and Procedures for a Workable System.* (New York, Oxford University Press) Ch 2

Haist, Matthew (2009) 'Deterrence in a Sea of Just Deserts: Are Utilitarian Goals Achievable in a World of Limiting Retributivism?' *Journal of Criminal Law Criminology* 99, 789.

Hudson, Barbara (2003), *Understanding Justice: An Introduction to Ideas, Perspectives and Controversies in Modern Penal Theory*, 2nd edn (Buckingham, Open University Press)

Morris, Norval and M Tonry (1991) *Between Prison and Probation: Intermediate Punishments in a Rational Sentencing System* (New York, Oxford University Press).

Morse, Stephen J (2011) 'Protecting Liberty and Autonomy: Desert/Disease Jurisprudence' *San Diego Law Review* 1077, 48.

Ryberg, Jesper (2011) 'Punishment and Desert-Adjusted Utilitarianism' in M Tonry (ed) *Retributivism Has a Past: Has It a Future?* (New York, Oxford University Press) Ch 5.

10

The Politics of the Desert Model

T HIS VOLUME, SO far, has addressed the substance of the desert model. I shall now turn, briefly, to questions of its politics. What general political outlook is presupposed by the desert-oriented conception of sentencing addressed in this volume? Do proportionalist sentencing policies lead to increased levels of punishment? Does desert theory divert attention from social ills? Let me try to address such questions here.

10.1 THE DESERT MODEL'S POLITICAL PEDIGREE

In penological thinking of the 1950s and 60s, retributivism was considered a conservative (indeed, a reactionary) idea. Symptomatic of that attitude was the proposed 'Model Sentencing Act', published in 1963 by the National Council on Crime and Delinquency (NCCD), a well-known liberal American penal-reform organisation.[1] According to the NCCD's proposed scheme, proportionality concerns would be excluded entirely from the determination of sentence; and rehabilitation and incapacitation would be the sole guiding aims. As a seemingly self-evident proposition, the draft Act states that 'sentences should not be based on revenge and retribution'.[2] While the drafters of this model legislation required that only offenders deemed likely to return to crime were to be imprisoned, the Act proposed giving sentencing judges the broadest discretion to impose lengthy prison sentences on any offender deemed likely to reoffend.[3] The drafters evidently did not see any risk to liberty involved creating such sweeping powers of resorting to imprisonment.

---

[1] National Council on Crime and Delinquency, Model Sentencing Act 1963.
[2] Ibid, s 1. This language assumes that retribution is the same as revenge.
[3] Ibid. Model Sentencing Act, ss 1, 5, 9.

The desert model—that is, the renewed interest in the idea of proportionality of sentence—emerged in the late 1970s among liberal penologists, in part as a response to this kind of thinking. Fair sentences, it began to be argued, should reflect the degree of seriousness of the criminal conduct. Substantial prison terms should not deemed to be the punishment which any potential recidivist should receive, but only those convicted offenders whose criminal conduct was serious. Proportionate sentences were advocated as a way of making penalties more just.

My 1976 book *Doing Justice*[4] took this approach. It was written on behalf of the Committee for the Study of Incarceration, a group (primarily of academics) with liberal sympathies. The principle of proportionality was offered as a means for *restricting* the state's authority to punish—particularly, as a way of limiting the use of prison sanctions. Predictively-based punishments were opposed—not only because they failed to fairly reflect the degree of reprehensibleness of the criminal conduct, but also because they would permit intervention, with few principled limits, into the lives of supposedly higher-risk offenders. Other penological writings of that era advocating the desert model had a similar tenor.[5]

During the decade of the 1970s, there was also extensive Nordic writing on sentence proportionality—exemplified by the collection of essays by Swedish, Finnish and Norwegian penologists, *Straff och rattfardighet* ('Punishment and Justice').[6] In these essays, the principle of proportionality was advocated as a *fair* response to crime, and modest penalty levels were also supported.

Recent penological writings on desert generally have maintained this tenor.[7] The principle of proportionality is defended chiefly on grounds

---

[4] A von Hirsch, *Doing Justice: The Choice of Punishments* (New York, Hill and Wang, 1976; Reprinted 1986 (Boston, Northeastern University Press)).

[5] See eg A Ashworth, *Sentencing and Penal Policy* (London, Heinemanns, 1983).

[6] S Heckscher, et al (eds), *Straff och rättfärdighet: Ny nordisk debatt* (Stockholm, Norstedts, 1980), discussed in Ch 1, section 1.2.

[7] See A Ashworth, 'Criminal Justice and Deserved Sentences' (1989) *Criminal Law Review* 340; A von Hirsch, *Past or Future Crimes: Deservedness and Dangerousness in the Sentencing of Criminals* (New Brunswick, New Jersey, Rutgers University Press, 1985; United Kingdom edn 1986 (Manchester, Manchester University Press)); A von Hirsch, *Censure and Sanctions* (Oxford, Oxford University Press, 1993); AE Bottoms, 'Five Puzzles in von Hirsch's Theory' in A Ashworth and M Wasik (eds),

of fairness. Substantial prison terms are to be restricted to persons convicted of seriously reprehensible criminal conduct. Proportionate sentencing is not offered as a means of reducing crime rates. Indeed, desert theorists have evinced considerable scepticism about how much crime rates can be made to respond to sentencing policy.[8] Absent an ambitious crime-reduction agenda, those writing in this vein have had little incentive to support increased reliance on prison sanctions.

A noteworthy aspect of this writing is that it also rejects talionic conceptions of desert (see Chapter 3). Notions of 'paying back'— of inflicting on the offender as much suffering as he caused to his victim—is no part of the theory. The basis of the theory is censure— not harm-for-harm equivalence—and censure in punishment can be conveyed through levels of punishment that would be well below those involved in 'paying back' the harm (see Chapter 3).

In discussions in the Nordic countries, proportionalist perspectives was termed as 'neo-classicist',[9] but that can be a source of confusion. The label 'neo-classic' suggests that proportionalist sentencing theory essentially involves a return to the 'classical' penology of the late 1700s and early 1800s. It does not. Traditional penal classicism did advocate penalties graded according to the gravity of the offence—but principally on grounds of deterrence. The leading rationale was Bentham's, according to which graded penalties would help induce offenders to prefer less to more injurious crimes. Such rationale, however, would leave proportionality weak and exception-prone, as I have noted earlier (Chapter 4). Modern proportionality doctrine is based on a different rationale, emphasising censure and punishment's role in addressing the offender as moral agent. This rationale supports firmer and less exception-prone proportionality limits—as the forgoing chapters have also suggested.

Fundamentals of Sentencing Theory: Essays in Andrew von Hirsch (Oxford, Oxford University Press, 1998) Ch 3; A von Hirsch and A Ashworth, *Proportionate Sentencing: Exploring the Principles* (Oxford, Oxford University Press, 2005); T Hörnle, *Tatproportionale Strafzumessung* (Berlin, Duncker und Humblot, 1999).

[8] Ashworth 1989; von Hirsch 1985, Ch 15; for a fuller discussion of the limited potential of deterrent sentences, see AE Bottoms and A von Hirsch, 'The Crime-Preventive Impact of Penal Sanctions' in P Cane and HM Kritzer (eds), *The Oxford Handbook of Empirical Legal Studies* (Oxford, Oxford University Press, 2010) Ch 4, 98–106.

[9] See eg, several of the essays in Heckscher et al 1980.

However, the 1980s and the 1990s also witnessed the advent of a ferocious conservatism in criminal-justice policy, especially in the United States and England. Politicians gave much-increased emphasis to 'law and order' themes. Conservative penologists, especially some American writers on punishment policy such as James Q Wilson[10] and Ernest van den Haag,[11] urged 'realistic' (actually, tougher) sentencing strategies aimed at bringing down crime rates. Because these developments were occurring at the same time as a renewal of interest in the proportionality of sentence, some critics suggested that proportionalism must be a part of a repressive strategy for dealing with crime.[12]

Conservative penal theorists, such as Wilson, however, actually showed scant interest in notions of proportionality. He asserted that desert should be considered only in setting broad outer limits on permissible punishments. Within those limits, he argued, actual sentence levels should be decided chiefly by considerations of deterrence and incapacitation.[13] Ernest van den Haag, in his later writings, rejected the idea of desert altogether.[14] Another conservative American penal theorist, Dan Kahan, recommended humiliating punishments for convicted offenders, and rejected significant proportionality constraints.[15] The reason for those theorists' scepticism about proportionate sentencing is apparent enough (and indeed, it is the mirror image of liberals' reasons for support): that ideas of proportionality could limit the scope of crime prevention or other consequentialist strategies. Singling out high-risk offenders for extended confinement—a favourite theme of Wilson's[16]—would be restricted under desert theory as violative of ordinal proportionality. Exemplary deterrence strategies aimed at reducing the demand for drugs by penalising users and minor sellers harshly—a favourite theme of American drug warriors—would also run afoul proportionality requirements. When the aim of the sentencing policy

[10] JQ Wilson, *Thinking about Crime*, revised edn (New York, Basic Books, 1983).

[11] See E van den Haag, 'Punishment: Desert and Control' (1987) *Michigan Law Review* 85, 1250, rejecting any role for desert.

[12] See eg, J Reiman and S Headlee (1981), 'Marxism and Criminal Justice Policy' (1981) *Crime & Delinquency* 27, 24.

[13] Wilson 1983, Ch 6.

[14] van den Haag 1987.

[15] DM Kahan, Dan M. (1996), 'What Do Alternative Sanctions Mean?' (1996) *University of Chicago Law Review* 63, 591.

[16] Wilson 1983, Ch 8.

is simply that of stopping crime, proportionality constraints appear to be mere impediments.

10.2 LIMITING SEVERITY: DESERT vs PENAL UTILITARIANISM

Does proportionalist sentencing theory call for more or less punishment? Some critics assert that desert theory provides no definite answers: the principle of proportionality, it is claimed, demands merely that penalties should be graded to reflect the comparative gravity of offences.[17] While the theory thus might permit a reduction in punishment levels, it is said, it would not require this result; and indeed, it would allow a substantial overall escalation of penalties. Proportionalism, despite all its pretence to liberalism, assertedly might comport with harsh sentencing policies.

I believe that, in the foregoing chapters, I have responded to this objection. A desert theorist does not have to be agnostic on issues of deciding the penalty system's levels of severity. Moderation in penalty levels is needed in order to give the censure element in punishment a meaningful role. The higher overall penalty levels rise, the less the normative reasons for desistence supplied by penal censure will matter, and the more the system becomes essentially one of bare threats.[18]

The critic might reply that not all adherents of a policy of proportionate sentences would necessarily accept such a claim; and if they do not, the indeterminacy of desert theory remains. The objection, however, is then much weakened, becoming merely that a wholly different conception of desert might supply less reason for constraining a penalty system's degree of repressiveness. However, this risk—of a differing version of a theory leading to divergent conclusions—would seem endemic to almost virtually any conception of punishment one could devise. Indeed, I have offered reasons for rejecting certain alternative conceptions of desert—for example, the talionic perspective—in part because of their tendency to produce severe outcomes (see Chapter 3).

---

[17] See, eg, N Walker, *Why Punish?* (Oxford, Oxford University Press, 1991) 101–03; N Lacey and H Pickard, 'The Chimera of Proportionality: Institutionalising Limits on Punishment in Contemporary Social and Political Systems' (2015) *Modern Law Review* 78, 216.

[18] See more fully, ch 5 above. See also, von Hirsch 1993, Ch 5; von Hirsch and Ashworth 2005, Ch 9, 142–43.

To get a clearer sense of the possible links between the desert model and severity levels, it might be helpful to compare that theory with a major modern alternative, of penal utilitarianism. Which theory would provide greater (or lesser) constraints on penalty levels?

The most visible version of penal utilitarianism was once the treatment model: that criminal-justice policy (including sentencing) should foster the rehabilitation of the offender. Faith in rehabilitation—at least, as the primary sentencing aim—has much declined in recent decades.[19] With the eclipse of the rehabilitative ethic, however, penal utilitarianism has not disappeared—but merely has shifted emphasis to other crime-preventive strategies (notably, deterrence and incapacitation). If punishment cannot cure criminals, arguably, more 'realistic' ways of reducing crime might be relied upon: intimidating potential offenders and restraining convicted ones.

These deterrent and incapacitative strategies entail, however, a particular risk of sanction escalation. There exists not only a danger of overall penalty increases (if moderate doses of punishment fail to deter or incapacitate sufficiently, why not try much bigger dosages?); but especially, a danger of disproportionate escalation in sanctions for offenders targeted for special attention.[20] What makes such strategies so worrisome is their apparent common-sense appeal. While it is hard to imagine widely effective treatments, might not dangerous felons be separated from the community? Doubts have by now been cast on how well existing deterrence and incapacitation strategies could actually achieve ambitious crime-prevention objectives.[21] However, the utilitarian might suggest, what should prevent us from adopting such strategies once we became able to improve our crime-prevention techniques?

Desert theory provides principled grounds for resisting such suggestions. The theory's guiding conception, of proportionality, is grounded in claims about justice. Preventive efficacy—the impact of sentencing reform on crime rates—is *not* the theory's main criterion for success. If a desert model is implemented and does not lead to reduction in the

---

[19] See ch 1, above. See, however, FT Cullen and KE Gilbert, *Reaffirming Rehabilitation*, 2nd edn (London, Routledge, 2012), calling for 'reaffirming rehabilitation'. Also, T Ward and S Maruna, *Rehabilitation* (London, Routledge, 2007).

[20] See discussion of 'selective incapacitation' strategies in ch 1.

[21] Zimring and Hawkins, *Incapacitation: Penal Confinement and the Restraint of Crime* (Chicago, Chicago University Press, 1995); Bottoms and von Hirsch 2010, 113–20; see also, ch 1, section 1.4 above.

incidence of crime, this is not a mark of the scheme's failure. Indeed, most desert advocates (including myself), as noted earlier, have been sceptical about achieving significant crime reductions through changes in sentencing policy (see, Chapter 1).

Sentencing reforms relying on the desert model should be evaluated, instead, in terms of their success in scaling the penal response to crime-gravity. Because reducing the incidence of crime would no longer be the sole aim, the theory furnishes less temptation to escalate punishments in the hope of achieving entranced preventive impact. Indeed, the Minnesota sentencing commission reportedly opted for desert over incapacitation in drafting its standards, in part because it did not wish to present its scheme to the public as a crime-control device—and then, if crime rates continued to rise, to face increased pressure to resort to yet tougher preventive medicine.[22]

The criteria for desert also rule out the more frightening forms of penal utilitarianism, such as selective incapacitation. The latter strategy calls for the imposition of extended sentences on 'high risk' felons—namely those deemed likely to commit serious crimes repeatedly. Such schemes make extensive use of indicia of risk which have little bearing on crime gravity—such as early offending, drug abuse, and unemployment.[23] A proportionalist conception of sentencing would rule out such strategies in principle, because these would rely on factors so divergent from the blameworthiness of the criminal conduct; and also because (to achieve any significant preventive impact) these would call for such large disparities in the severity of sentences of defendants deemed dangerous, as compared with those others convicted of comparably reprehensible crimes.

An alternative approach that sometimes has been advocated is the revival of rehabilitation.[24] Treatment, it is said, is a more humane notion

---

[22] For recent analysis of Minnesota's sentencing guidelines, see RS Frase, *Just Sentencing: Principles and Procedures for a Workable System* (New York, Oxford University Press, 2013) 123–40.

[23] See National Academy of Sciences, Panel on Research on Criminal Careers, 'Criminal Careers and "Career Criminals"' (edited by A Blumstein, J Cohen, J Roth and C Visher) (Washington DC, National Academies of Sciences Press, 1986) Vol 1; von Hirsch 1985, Ch 11.

[24] Cullen and Gilbert 2012; see also, A von Hirsch, A Ashworth and JV Roberts (eds), *Principled Sentencing: Readings in Theory and Policy*, 3rd edn (Oxford, Hart Publishing, 2009) 28–38; Cullen and Gilbert 2012.

than deterrence or incapacitation; it is by now widely understood that the prison is seldom a cure for offenders' criminal tendencies. A return to rehabilitation, assertedly, would pave the way for less harsh penal policies. Ideologies cannot be revived at will, however. The rehabilitative ethic seemed so attractive in past decades, because it was believed that offenders could readily be cured of their criminal inclinations. That assertion scarcely rings plausible today: despite reported successes with some experimental programmes targeted at small groups of offenders, routine success with the bulk of convicted criminals has remained an elusive goal.[25]

The supposed intrinsic humaneness of treatment may also be questioned. The rehabilitative ethic offers few, if any, principled limits on how onerous penal therapies may be. Rehabilitationism has had worrisome embodiments in the past, such as lengthy, indeterminate terms of confinement for the sake of treatment.[26] Newer rehabilitative techniques may also be much less gentle than their proponents claim. Drug treatments, especially, can be very burdensome, involving compulsory residence in treatment facilities for significant durations.[27] The small-time drug seller, on a rehabilitative sentencing ethic, may face such onerous interventions as these—instead of the much lower penalties that a proportionalist sentencing scheme would propose for lesser crimes.

The desert-oriented model proposed in this volume is not premised, however, on any general rejection of rehabilitation or social service for convicted offenders. Thus:

— Social service consists of programmes aimed at making the quality of life better for convicted offenders, and at offsetting some of the social deficits that many such offenders would suffer as a result of being punished. Programmes of skill-training, education, and psychological assistance are examples. These should be broadly available to offenders on a voluntary basis. A proportionalist sentencing

---

[25] See Bottoms and von Hirsch 2010, 108–13.

[26] Nordic examples include the former Swedish internment system and the Danish regime of lengthy, indefinite sentences, formerly imposed at the treatment facility at Haerstedvester.

[27] D Husak, Douglas, 'Retributivism, Proportionality, and the Challenge of the Drug Court Movement' in M Tonry (ed), *Retributivism Has a Past; Has it a Future?* (New York, Oxford University Press, 2011) Ch 11.

rationale would not restrict the use of such programmes, so long as the severity of sentence is not thereby increased (as it ordinarily would not be).

— Programmes that are rehabilitative, in the traditional sense of the term, are aimed at reducing offenders' likelihood of recidivism. These may or may not affect the choice of sentence. Where they do not—as in the case of treatments offered during the duration of a prison sentence—no issue of proportionality is raised. Where they do affect that choice—eg, where a sentence of one type is chosen over another type because it better permits a course of treatment— then its appropriateness under a desert rationale depends upon whether the two types of sentence are of approximately comparable intrusiveness or not. What desert theory restricts, however, is increasing the severity of the penalty on treatment grounds: for example, imposing imprisonment instead of a fine or conditional sentence, because the offender could then be placed in a prison-based treatment programme (see more fully, Chapter 8 above).

A good test of the comparative merits of desert and utilitarian models concerns their applicability to intermediate sanctions. There have been two major problems with developing such non-custodial measures. First, the temptation exists to employ middle-level sanctions against lesser offenders, because such persons are perceived as potentially more cooperative recruits into treatment programmes. Second, imprisonment may be invoked as the penalty for those who commit technical breaches of the terms of their community penalty, thereby ultimately increasing reliance on imprisonment. Desert theory does offer principled responses here, as we have seen: the more onerous non-custodial sanctions may not be employed for lower-ranking crimes, and there would be substantial limits on breach penalties (Chapter 8 above). Utilitarian theories, however, offer no such limits: for example, a breach of the conditions of a treatment programme could be treated as an indicator of increased risk that would justify a lengthy stint of incarceration.

10.3 PROPORTIONALITY AND INCREASED SEVERITY?

Critics of desert theory have claimed that proportionalist sentencing conceptions more generally legitimate increased use of imprisonment. By emphasising the offence, they assert, desert theory supports the creation of mechanical schemes such as the US Sentencing Guideline Commission's numerical guidelines,[28] which prescribe penalties of imprisonment for a large number of Federal crimes. Such mechanical schemes assertedly increase the 'distance' between the judge and the offender, and thereby lead to harsh penalties being more readily inflicted.[29]

This account is untenable. The US Sentencing Commission did *not* rely on desert principles in fashioning its undoubtedly severe sentencing standards and, indeed, rejected such ideas explicitly, as permitting insufficient scope for deterrent and incapacitative aims.[30] Certain US states, most notably Minnesota, have adopted numerical guidelines which do rely on the idea of proportionality—but such schemes tend to have modest rates of imprisonment by American standards.[31] Notwithstanding claims that the Federal scheme and Minnesota's guidelines have 'the same principles behind their work', the rationales of such schemes are actually very different, as are their degrees of reliance on imprisonment.[32]

When we turn from the US to the Nordic countries, assertions about the desert model's supposed baleful influence become still more

---

[28] For a sketch of these guidelines, see Frase 2013, 163–64.

[29] See, eg J Braithwaite and P Pettit, *Not Just Deserts: A Republican Theory of Justice* (Oxford, Oxford University Press, 1990).

[30] US Sentencing Commission, *Federal Sentencing Guidelines Manual* (Washington DC, US Sentencing Commission, 1987) 60–64; see also, A von Hirsch, 'Federal Sentencing Guidelines: Do They Provide Principled Guidance?' (1989) *American Criminal Law Review* 27, 367; A Doob, 'The United States Sentencing Commission Guidelines' in C Clarkson and R Morgan (eds), *The Politics of Sentencing Reform* (Oxford, Oxford University Press, 1995), Ch 6.

[31] For description and analysis of these states' sentencing guidelines, see Frase 2013, Ch 3; A von Hirsch, 'Proportionality and Parsimony in American Sentencing Guidelines: The Minnesota and Oregon Standards' in CMV Clarkson and R Morgan (eds), *The Politics of Sentencing Reform* (Oxford, Oxford University Press, 1995) 149, Ch 6.

[32] The Canadian criminologist Anthony Doob (1995) provided an extensive analysis of the Federal sentencing guidelines and their structure. Doob concludes that the guidelines reflect no consistent substantive rationale; for example, they provide a much heavier emphasis on the criminal record than a desert rationale would, and make no effort to rate the seriousness of crimes in systematic fashion. There is also no sustained attempt even to pursue crime prevention rationale (say, selective incapacitation). Doob concludes that the guidelines' principal purpose was to increase severity levels in one fashion or another, for essentially political purposes of showing severity toward convicted criminals.

implausible. The two Nordic nations which have adopted proportionalist sentencing policies (namely, Finland and Sweden) did so via statutory statements of principle, rather than numerical tables of sentences.
Finland enacted its sentencing statute in 1976, which calls for sentences
'in just proportion' to the gravity of the criminal conduct.[33] Sweden
put into effect its present sentencing law, which relies on similar ideas
but in fuller detail, a decade later, in 1989.[34] If the critics' contentions
were correct, one would expect these enactments to have led to sharp
increases in imprisonment rates, in comparison to the other Nordic
countries which did not adopt comparable legislation. But there has
been no evidence of this.

Indeed, Finland has achieved the greatest relative decline in incarceration levels among the Nordic nations—and did so during the
period just after the enactment of its proportionality-oriented sentencing law in 1976.[35] Granted, Finland started with higher imprisonment
levels than its Nordic neighbours, but if claims about the escalatory
influence of the desert model in sentencing were correct, those high
levels would have been raised still higher. The Swedish sentencing-
reform law of 1988 was designed to be neutral in its impact on rates
of imprisonment.[36] Since then, there has been some increase in levels
of imprisonment—due mainly to changes to the rules on drink-driving,
and problems with the norms of parole eligibility.[37] But such increases
have been modest,[38]—rather than large, as desert-theory's critics would
anticipate. Given the general upward trends in imprisonment levels in
most Western countries in recent decades—reflecting public fears of

---

[33] Finnish Penal Code, Ch 6. For discussion of Finland's and Sweden's sentencing schemes, see ch 1 above.

[34] Swedish Penal Code, Chs 29, 30.

[35] T Lappi-Seppälä, *Regulating the Prison Population: Experiences from a Long-Term
Policy in Finland* (Helsinki, National Research Institute of Legal Policy, 1998);
T Lappi-Seppälä, 'Penal Policy in Scandinavia' in M Tonry (ed), *Crime, Punishment,
and Politics in a Comparative Perspective. Crime and Justice* (Chicago, Chicago University
Press, 2007) Vol 36.

[36] See the Swedish Government report introducing the legislation, Regerings
Proposition 1987/88, 120; N Jareborg, 'The Swedish Sentencing Reform' in
C Clarkson and R Morgan (eds), *The Politics of Sentencing Reform* (Oxford, Oxford
University Press, 1995).

[37] See eg Jareborg 1995.

[38] Estimates of the impact on prison populations have been provided in
Jareborg 1995.

crime and disorder and a greater politicisation of sentencing issues—having just modest increases is, perhaps, the most favourable outcome that realistically could have been hoped for.

Claims about the baleful influence of proportionalism rest on characterising as desert-driven any sentencing approach which reduces sentencing discretion and gives diminished emphasis to rehabilitation. As numerous jurisdictions have made such changes, that would suggest that the desert model has swept the world and must be responsible for rising levels of imprisonment. But the desert model involves more than guidance for sentencing. It means guidance of a certain kind: that which emphasises proportionate sanctions, based on the degree of seriousness of the criminal conduct. Thus defined, only a limited number of jurisdictions have adopted this approach in systematic fashion: as noted previously, Finland and Sweden (and, to a lesser degree, England) in Europe; and Minnesota and Oregon in the US; and recently Israel.[39] Careful analysis of the reforms in those places will show they were designed to *limit* increases in the use of imprisonment.[40]

10.4 'LAW AND ORDER' STRATEGIES

The decades of the 1980s and 90s witnessed a proliferation of 'law and order' responses to crime. These involved strident rhetoric about crime and criminals, and called for drastic increases in criminal sanctions. A notorious example was California's 'three strikes' law, adopted in 1984, calling for mandatory prison terms of 25 years to life imprisonment for third convictions of numerous types of felonies, including intermediate-level offences such as burglary.[41] Comparable populist appeals to law and order were also heard, in England.

Until the early 1980s, England had not paid much attention to sentencing-reform issues. During that decade, however, extensive interest developed in proportionality of sentence and techniques for guiding

---

[39] See ch 1, nn 8–9.

[40] See section 10.2 above.

[41] For discussion of this statute, see FE Zimring, G Hawkins and S Kamin, *Punishment and Democracy: Three Strikes and You're Out in California* (New York, Oxford University Press, 2001). In one much publicised case, a defendant with two prior burglary convictions received virtual life imprisonment for a third offence of having snatched a slice of pizza from a child.

sentencing discretion. In 1990, the Government published a major policy paper advocating systematic sentencing reform, and proposing that proportionality should be the primary criterion for deciding both the use of imprisonment and the use of non-custodial sentences.[42] The document suggested that proportionality criteria could help reduce reliance on imprisonment, by restricting the use of imprisonment for repetitive minor property offenders. This proposal evolved, with various amendments, into the Criminal Justice Act 1991—that made proportionality the main criterion governing the choice both of custodial and non-custodial sentences.[43] During the initial months after the coming into force of the Act, rates of imprisonment did decline significantly.[44]

However, the political mood then changed—with law-and-order becoming a major theme for both major English political parties. Attacks upon the proportionality-oriented 1991 Criminal Justice Act as unduly liberal began to be voiced, along with demands by influential political figures for harsher punishments. By 1994, the Government adopted legislation watering down the 1991 Act's restrictions on sentencing courts' relying on offenders' previous criminal histories.[45] A strongly right-wing Home Secretary (interior minister), Michael Howard, took office the same year, claiming that 'prison works' and urging judges to impose much harsher sentences. In 1997, shortly before the end of the Conservative Government, Howard secured the passage of mandatory minimum sentence laws,[46] requiring lengthy custodial sentences for third convictions of drug-dealing, and at least three-year custodial sentences for third-time burglary convictions. After the general election of that year, the new Labour Home Secretary, Jack Straw, took over many of his predecessor's law-and-order themes, and put these mandatory minimum sentences into effect.[47]

---

[42] UK Government White Paper, *Crime, Justice and Protecting the Public* (London, HMSO, 1990).

[43] Criminal Justice Act 1993.

[44] A Ashworth, *Sentencing and Criminal Justice*, 6th edn (Cambridge, Cambridge University Press, 2015) 100–06.

[45] Crime (Sentences) Act 1994.

[46] Crime (Sentences) Act 1997.

[47] Those events are described in Lord Windlesham's excellent historical account, D Windlesham, *Responses to Crime* (New York, Oxford University Press, 1996) Vol 3.

Such 'populist punitiveness' has little in common with proportionalist sentencing conceptions, however. Singling out middle-level convicted offenders for long mandatory prison terms, manifestly countervenes proportionality requirements—and, indeed, 'law-and-order' advocates were explicit in their disdain to the desert model. But such 'get tough' measures also had scant plausibility as crime prevention measures. When Michael Howard introduced his mandatory minimum sentences for drug-dealing and burglary, he merely asserted that they would help reduce the incidence of these crimes, but offered no calculations or other evidence of the measures' likely preventive effects.[48] His Labour successor as Home Secretary, Jack Straw, put the measures into force, notwithstanding having himself commissioned a criminological study which had questioned the effectiveness of such measures as a deterrent.[49] Three strikes also seemed deficient as an incapacitative strategy, because offenders would usually receive their third 'strike' conviction late in their expected criminal careers, when their most active phase of offending was likely to have passed.[50]

If law-and-order strategies appear to show so little concern either for proportionality or for crime-prevention effectiveness, what has been their aim? It appears to be that of appealing to and mobilising popular resentment, through the advocacy and adoption of drastic sanctions. Such appeals do have an instrumental function, but not a substantive one. Exploiting popular resentment is a way—sometimes, unhappily,

[48] This claim appeared in a 1996 government White Paper, asserting that the adoption of the proposed mandatory minimum sentence for burglary would reduce burglary rates by 20%. However, the Home Office did not supply any evidence for this claim.

[49] When taking office in 1997, Straw deferred putting into effect the three-year mandatory minimum sentence for burglary of the Crime (Sentences) Act 1997, and announced he was commissioning a review of recent deterrence research, before deciding on implementation. The contract to conduct such a review was awarded to the Institute of Criminology at Cambridge University—which in 1999 submitted a report concluding that there was little or no evidence of enhanced marginal deterrence through increased sentence severity; see A von Hirsch, A Bottoms et al, *Criminal Deterrence and Sentence Severity: An Analysis of Recent Research* (Oxford, Hart Publishing, 1999). Shortly after having received that report, Mr Straw decided to put the mandatory minimum for burglary into effect nevertheless.

[50] See more fully, FE Zimring and G Hawkins, *Incapacitation: Penal Confinement and the Restraint of Crime* (Oxford, Oxford University Press, 1995) Ch 8.

an effective way—for garnering political support. Modern society can provide fertile grounds for such appeals. Crime is a highly visible (and very troubling) social phenomenon, made all the more so by the manner in which it is reported in the media. Modern living also has manifold other frustrations, for which crime can serve as an apt symbol. Appeals to resentment can tap these sources of ill-feeling.

Can law-and-order strategies be seen as a species of communicative punishment? If communication is involved, it is of a very different kind. Criminals are to be given harsh sentences in order to give public expression to the contempt with which such persons are to be regarded. On this view, it would not be necessary (as desert theorists hold) to make the penalty proportionate to the seriousness of the crime; nor (as preventionists would hold) to ensure that penalties actually are more effective in reducing crime. The emphasis, instead, would be on giving public and official voice to animus against crime and criminals.[51]

On the desert model, disapprobation is visited on the offender, perceived as a person capable of moral agency. Certain conduct is deemed harmful and blameworthy, and the sanction should convey a measure of disapprobation for it. How much the actor is penalised thus should comport with the degree of reprehensibleness of his behaviour. Since the censure for the conduct is being conveyed through the medium of penal deprivation, the severity of the sanctions should reflect the seriousness of his conduct, and not more: hence, the requirements of proportionality (see Chapters 3 and 4).

On the law-and-order version of denunciation, however, the convicted offenders' punishment would serve as the mere conduit for a public message of opprobrium. If escalating penalty levels would best express this message, it is deemed preferable—and the offender is to be disallowed any standing to claim that the sanction overstates the blame due him. Such a perspective is ethically unacceptable; it certainly is not one implied by, or even minimally consistent with, desert theory.

---

[51] For a description and critique of penal-populist strategies such as Straw's and Blunkett's, see M Tonry, *Punishment and Politics: Evidence and Emulation in the Making of English Crime Control Policy* (Cullompton, Willan Publishing, 2004); N Lacey, *The Prisoner's Dilemma: Political Economy and Punishment in Contemporary Democracies* (Cambridge, Cambridge University Press, 2008).

10.5 ARGUMENTS ABOUT 'UNDERLYING ILLS'

Another cluster of criticisms of desert theory has concerned its supposed failure to address certain fundamental ills, such as the underlying social causes of crime. Let me consider these objections briefly.

1. Proportionalist sentencing doctrine is sometimes said to blame the offender for harm that is really society's fault. Bad social conditions, it is asserted, are actually responsible for crime (or at least for its high incidence). The desert rationale diverts attention from remedying these social conditions, by focussing on the wrongful behaviour of convicted offenders—whose crimes may stem from their own social victimisation.

These are apt criticisms of conservative utilitarian theories, such as those of the late James Q Wilson. In a much-quoted passage, Wilson argued that government is not in a position to remedy fundamental social ills; and moreover, that it need not try to do so, because crime can more efficiently be dealt with through rigorous crime-prevention measures.[52] Thus, his prescriptions for preserving public order would come at the expense of efforts to alleviate social injustice.

This is *not* a position that the desert theory holds, however. A modern state should be capable, at least to a degree, of alleviating poverty and social disorganisation, and the European states that have made substantial efforts in this direction have had a measure of success. Nor would I concur with Wilson's view that it is possible, without trying to alleviate social misery, to reduce crime merely through this or that crime prevention technique. It is no accident that Stockholm or Berlin are safer than Dallas or Los Angeles, and the reasons relate more to the extent of social deprivation in those latter places than to criminal-justice efficiency.

Sentencing policy is not a good tool for reducing criminality or promoting wider social justice. If we want a more equitable society, we will need to maintain and pay for the requisite schemes of social assistance. That might help shrink criminogenic conditions in the community, at least to a degree.

The sentencing of convicted persons, however, cannot wait until underlying social ills are remedied, nor can it be abandoned once they are addressed. Crime (including crime of a serious nature) will occur

---

[52] See, Wilson 1983, Ch 6.

in any event. So the question is unavoidable: when convicted offenders face sentence, what guiding rationale could help assure that these decisions are made justly—or at least, with the minimum of injustice? Addressing fundamental social ills (desirable as this is) cannot constitute a substitute for trying to make sentencing policy fairer and more coherent.

The Swedish and Finnish experience illustrates this point. Both countries have had for decades an extensive network of state-financed social welfare programmes, ranging from unemployment insurance through health care to child support. These measures have doubtless helped reduce want; and the wide sharing of prosperity may well have contributed to the relatively low levels of violence and disorder in those countries. Crime has not disappeared in those countries, however—nor with it the need for a workable sentencing policy. Finland and Sweden switched to a desert-oriented sentencing framework, because that was felt to provide clearer and fairer guidance. The adoption of these laws, however, certainly was not premised on rejection of larger social welfare supports. If one were to ask the drafters of the Finnish or Swedish statutes whether these laws 'addressed' the country's remaining social ills, their answer would be certainly not—because that is the proper task of social-welfare measures, not criminal-justice legislation.

2. Desert theorists do assert that even if their recommended sentencing policies cannot cure social disadvantage, it at least does not leave disadvantaged offenders *worse* off. The factors gauging crime-seriousness (and hence the severity of the penalty) concern primarily the conduct's harmfulness and the actor's degree of culpability; social factors (such as employment status, education, age, etc) generally carry little or no weight. Desert thus is preferable in this respect to utilitarian strategies such as selective incapacitation, because the latter explicitly allow reliance upon social factors in a manner that put badly-off defendants in a *worse* position when they face sentence—with factors such as unemployment, lack of skills, and unstable residence serving to increase penalties, as indicia of risk.[53]

---

[53] B Hudson, *Justice through Punishment: A Critique of the 'Justice' Model of Corrections* (London, St Martins, 1987). Hudson later formulated a view that would generally adopt desert-oriented standards, but which provided mitigation for socially deprived offenders; B Hudson, 'Doing Justice to Difference' in A Ashworth and

A desert perspective is in no way premised on a rejection of providing social welfare to citizens. The approach is liberal, in the sense that it seeks to place limits on the coercive powers of the state. But it is not 'neo-liberal' in the sense of seeking to limit the state's role in providing social assistance. Support of proportionality requirements in punishment does not presuppose adoption of any general view that distribution of social benefits by the state should be scaled back. The penal desert perspective rests on the special character of a punishment in conveying blame or censure: a blaming institution, the theory holds, should have its impositions distributed according to criminal actors' fault. Social benefits and welfare support, however, are neutral in character—they convey neither praise nor blame, and thus may be distributed universally or (as the case may be) according to need, without regard to the supposed merit of those affected. A penal desert theorist thus can favour (as I emphatically do) extensive programmes of education, health, and income support.

A consistent perspective is needed, here. One might begin with something like an ideal perspective: of what sentencing policies there should look like in a just (or at least, not manifestly unjust) social and economic order. In such an environment, much can be said in favour of desert theorists' view that punishment ought to chiefly reflect the degree of blameworthiness of the conduct, rather than social-status factors. There might be some exceptions, for those social factors that seem to bear directly on the blameworthiness of the criminal conduct. Martin Gardner, an American criminal law scholar, has thus suggested that extreme want reduces the culpability of the actor in committing a criminal act, and hence should be treated as an extenuating circumstance.[54] Assuming the society had relatively small pockets of deprivation, such exceptions could be invoked infrequently. Andrew Ashworth and I thus have suggested the possibility of penalty reductions for seriously deprived offenders—albeit on somewhat different grounds.[55] There remain, however, difficult problems of fashioning workable legal principles that could implement such an extenuating ground.

M Wasik (eds), *Fundamentals of Sentencing Theory: Essays in Honour of Andrew von Hirsch* (Oxford, Oxford University Press, 1998) Ch 9.

[54] M Gardner, 'The Renaissance of Retribution: In Examination of "Doing Justice"' (1976) *Wisconsin Law Review* 781.

[55] von Hirsch and Ashworth 2005, Ch 5.

Next, one could focus on the realities of many Western countries, in which deprivation is much more extensive and the deprived are at a real disadvantage in the legal process. There, however, it would be especially hazardous to urge heavy reliance on social factors in sentencing policy. If crime rates are high, there will be great difficulty securing the adoption in sentencing law of poverty-based mitigating factors that would diminish punishments for a large number of low-income convicted offenders. Increased use of social-status factors is likely to produce just the opposite effect: of introducing risk-considerations that make indigent defendants worse off, still. What one must not do, however, is to try to have it both ways: criticise the use of desert factors from a 'realistic' perspective, and at the same time urge adoption of other, 'non-legal' ones for immediate use, from a utopian viewpoint.

10.6 THE 'VACUOUSNESS' ARGUMENT

A final objection to be addressed is the 'vacuousness' argument, made by Nicola Lacey and Hanna Pickard in a recent *Modern Law Review* article.[56] These authors' objection to the desert model is that its principle of proportionality is 'chimerical', because it furnishes no workable mediating norms linking its crime-seriousness scale with the scale of punishments.[57] Imagine, thus, a draconian version of 'deserved' punishments, in which all crimes would receive prison sentences—from the least serious (perhaps, punishable by several months' imprisonment) to the most serious (punishable, say, by life sentences). Why would such an inflated scale not also qualify as 'proportionate'?

This objection is untenable, because a desert-oriented penalty scale is not to be constructed in such a purely comparative fashion. According to the scheme outlined in this volume, crime-seriousness would be gauged in terms of the criminal conduct's impact on victims' and potential victims' living standards, as defined through Amartya Sen's

---

[56] Lacey and Pickard 2015.

[57] Although Lacey and Pickard do not address a penalty scale's anchoring points specifically, they do argue that the criteria of proportionality would permit an inflation of the scale: 'The notion of proportionality generates in itself no concrete limits to punishment; hence the question of how much—and indeed how—to punish remains open to the sway of convention, political decision, or expediency.' (Ibid, 235).

notion of standardised quality of life (see Chapter 6). This would generate anchoring norms for the scale—for example, that only serious crimes (as thus defined in Sen's quality-of-life terms) could warrant severe punishments such as lengthy prison terms (see also Chapter 8). The model also makes use of various other anchoring points—for example, those concerning the 'in-out' boundary between imprisonment and intermediate sanctions (see Chapter 7).

A desert-based scheme should also be influenced by assumptions concerning the political and social context. That is why, in my discussion here, I draw my examples from a particular setting: one having strong liberal traditions, Sweden. In different settings, the specifics of the penalty scheme may have to be developed somewhat differently—although the reasons for such differences would need to be explained. The problem with Lacey's and Pickard's objection is, essentially, that it posits a stripped-down notion of proportionality and then (unsurprisingly) finds that to be vacuous.

For further reading:

Ashworth, Andrew (2015) *Sentencing and Criminal Justice* 6th edn (Cambridge, Cambridge University Press, 2015) Chs 4, 6, 9.

Reitz, Kevin R (2006) 'Don't Blame Determinacy: US Incarceration Growth Has Been Driven by Other Forces' *Texas Law Review* 84, 1787.

Tonry, Michael (ed) (2014) *Crime and Justice (Vol 43): Why Crime Rates Fall, and Why They Don't* (New York, Oxford University Press).

Zimring, Franklin E, G Hawkins and S Kamin (2001) *Punishment and Democracy: Three Strikes and You're Out in California* (New York, Oxford University Press).

11

Proportionate Sentences for Juveniles

11.1 INTRODUCTION

THERE ARE GREATER contrasts among Western European countries' approaches to juvenile justice than among those for adult criminal justice.[1] Some countries (eg, Sweden) have a justice system for juveniles emphasising on proportionality of sentence.[2] Youthful offenders are tried in the same courts as adult offenders, and the severity of their sentences depends in important part (as it does in Sweden for adults) on the degree of seriousness of the actor's criminal offence. The salient difference in the treatment of juvenile offenders lies in its reduced penalty levels: the onerousness of sentences for juveniles is substantially scaled down, compared with those for adults.[3] Other European jurisdictions have adopted quite varying approaches. England, in its Sentencing Guidelines Council's recently promulgated standards for sentencing youths, has a desert-orientated approach[4] bearing significant similarities to Sweden's. Scotland, by contrast, has adopted a rehabilitation-oriented scheme for sentencing young offenders.[5] Other countries (eg, Germany)[6] have hybrid systems, employing a mixed set of aims.

---

[1] For a survey of such contrasting approaches, see BC Feld and DM Bishop (eds), *The Oxford Handbook of Juvenile Crime and Juvenile Justice* (New York, Oxford University Press, 2012).

[2] See also, A von Hirsch and A Ashworth, *Proportionate Sentencing: Exploring the Principles* (Oxford, Oxford University Press, 2005) Ch 3.

[3] N Jareborg, 'The Swedish Sentencing Reform' in C Clarkson and R Morgan (eds), *The Politics of Sentencing Reform* (Oxford, Oxford University Press, 1995).

[4] See Sentencing Guidelines Council (England and Wales), *Overarching Principles—Sentencing Youths* (London, Sentencing Guidelines Council, 2009).

[5] M Hill, A Lockyer and F Stone (eds), *Youth Justice and Child Protection* (London, Jessica Kingsley, 2007).

[6] While the German juvenile court act generally gives principal emphasis to rehabilitation, its provisions on the grounds for incarcerating juveniles refer to

There have been, in the Anglo-American literature of juvenile justice and particularly in the writings of two of America's leading juvenile-justice scholars, Barry Feld and Franklin Zimring, suggestions that emphasis should, as a matter of fairness, be given to the degree of seriousness of a juvenile offender's criminal conduct.[7] These authors also advocate that proportionate sentences for juveniles should be scaled down, well below those applicable to adult offenders (as is already the case in Sweden).

I am in general agreement with the Swedish approach—and also with the views of Feld and Zimring, that penalties for juveniles should be proportionate with the seriousness of offences; but that the criteria for proportionality should prescribe significantly reduced penalties compared with those for adults.[8] The present chapter explores the reasons why this should be the policy.

We might begin with a hypothetical sentencing scheme for adults, based on a rationale of proportionate, deserved sentences outlined in the previous chapters. In such a scheme, penalties would be graded according to the seriousness of the offences involved, with a modest adjustment for an offender's previous convictions. The scheme's underlying rationale would emphasise penal censure, rather than 'paying back' the offender for his offence. The scheme thus would employ moderate penalties, as discussed above (Chapter 5).

With such a scheme in mind, the question I shall address here is how such a scheme should be modified when applied to juvenile offenders.[9] The thesis I will defend is that substantial overall penalty reductions would be called for, in comparison with sentences for adults.[10] The

---

other factors, including incapacitation (that the offender has 'dangerous inclinations') and desert (his offence is serious).

[7] FE Zimring, *The Changing Legal World of Adolescence* (New York, Free Press, 1982); B Feld, *Bad Kids: Race and the Transformation of the Juvenile Court* (New York, Oxford University Press, 1999); B Feld, 'Adolescent Criminal Responsibility, Proportionality, and Sentencing Policy' (2012) *Law & Inequality* 31, 263.

[8] See also L Zedner, 'Sentencing Young Offenders' in A Ashworth and M Wasik (eds), *Fundamentals of Sentencing Theory* (Oxford, Oxford University Press, 1998) Ch 7.

[9] Juvenile offenders, for purposes of the present analysis, would be those whose ages range from the minimum age of criminal responsibility up to those of legal adulthood.

[10] In some jurisdictions, however, juveniles now may not be entitled to any penalty reduction at all. In various American states, juveniles whose cases have

amount of those reductions should be graded according to young offenders' age. The issue then becomes *why* this should be appropriate. The available literature refers to three kinds of reasons for punishing juveniles less severely: (1) juveniles' reduced culpability; (2) criminal sanctions' greater 'punitive bite' when applied to juveniles; and (3) the notion of adolescence as a 'time of testing'. Each of these three themes will be addressed here.[11]

11.2 CULPABILITY

An argument for reduced punishments that has surfaced in the juvenile-justice literature concerns young offenders on a reduced degree of culpability. If a 15-year-old commits burglary, or if a 30-year-old commits it, the harmful consequences of the criminal act would be the same; but what should differ are ascriptions of culpability: the juvenile acts with less personal fault in committing the act, rendering the behaviour less serious. Thus, there should be comparatively less punishment for the crime, because it is less serious than a comparable criminal act committed by an adult.

The question then becomes, *why* is culpability reduced? Two kinds of arguments have been put forward in the literature: (1) a *cognitive* claim, that juveniles have less capacity to assess and appreciate the harmful consequences of their criminal actions; and (2) a claim concerning *volitional controls*, that they have less opportunity to develop impulse control and resist peer pressure to offend. But *why* should these factors be permitted to count as culpability-reducing? For a sane adult, insufficiently developed impulse control is not ordinarily considered grounds of reduced culpability. Why should it be otherwise for juveniles?

been 'waived' to the adult court may face adult levels of punishment. Indeed, juveniles as young as 13 years of age have been sentenced to life imprisonment without parole.

[11] For discussion of these and related factors, see also ES Scott and L Steinberg, 'Blaming Youth' (2002) *Texas Law Review* 81, 799; RA Bierschbach, 'Proportionality and Parole' (2012) *University of Pennsylvania Law Review* 160, 1745; BC Feld, 'Youth Discount: Old Enough to Do the Crime, Too Young to Do the Time' (2013) *Ohio State Journal of Criminal Law* 11, 107.

11.2a Cognitive Factors

The cognitive claim relates to juveniles' lesser capacity to grasp the harmful effects of their actions. Adolescents, it is said, 'have not acquired the capacity to realise as fully as adults the consequences of their actions'.[12] But what kinds of consequences are being referred to here?

This deficiency of knowledge would not ordinarily concern those consequences that constitute the defining elements of the crime. Many commonplace offences committed by juveniles require purpose or knowledge on the part of the defendant. For residential burglary, for example, a person satisfies the act requirements of the offence if he unlawfully enters the dwelling of another in order to take property belonging to that person. He must, however, be aware that the dwelling and the property are not his own; and must have had, when entering the dwelling, the intention to take the property nevertheless. If he does not understand such matters, he is not committing burglary at all. However, simple knowledge of this kind is something that most juveniles are capable of having. Even a 15-year-old, when he breaks into an apartment and steals a television set, ordinarily can grasp that the flat is someone else's and that the television should not be his for the taking.

In what other respects, then, may the juvenile be said to have less appreciation of the act's harmful consequences? That reduced awareness concerns the role and importance of the interests which the prohibition is designed to protect. The prohibition against residential burglary relates to unauthorised entry into the dwelling of another for purposes of committing a theft or other offence. But what interests are thereby protected? Prevention of theft could not be the sole aim, as that is dealt with by other criminal prohibitions. Prevention of trespass into the homeowner's property also cannot be a sufficient explanation, as trespass is likewise dealt with by another prohibition. In a burglary, the paramount interests at stake, it would seem, relate to personal privacy and the sense of personal security. It is with respect to

---

[12] C Ball, K McCormac and N Stone, *Young Offenders: Law, Policy and Practice* (London, Sweet & Maxwell, 1995) 115; see also, Feld 1999 306–12; FE Zimring, 'Toward a Jurisprudence of Youth Violence' in M Tonry and M Moore (eds), *Youth Violence. Criminal Justice*: A Review of Research (Chicago, Chicago University Press, 1999) Vol 24, 487.

consequences of this kind, that juveniles' understanding may be insufficient. While the 15-year-old house burglar may be fully aware that he has entered his victim's flat illegally in order to take a television set that is not rightly his, he may have less grasp of how his intrusion infringes the victim's legitimate sense of the dwelling as his own personal space, and of how his unwanted entry can make that person feel vulnerable and insecure. And even if he comprehends these matters factually, he still may not properly *appreciate* them—that is, have a sense of (say) what it might feel like to have one's living space thus invaded.

What remains to be explained, however, is why this kind of incomplete comprehension of the relevant interests should affect the ascription of fault. For adults, such considerations would usually not be considered exculpating or even mitigating: the 35-year-old house burglar who thinks he is merely trespassing and stealing a few items of personal property is not considered to merit less punishment in virtue of the fact that he fails to appreciate the character of the privacy invasion which his conduct involves. We demand of a competent adult a general understanding of other people's basic interests, and of how various kinds of misconduct could intrude upon such interests.[13] Lack of understanding of such matters constitutes a failure to possess the relevant moral standards, and should not be extenuating; the house burglar who lacks this kind of comprehension is not thought preferable, morally speaking, to the burglar who does understand and enters and steals anyway.

If the conclusion should be different for juveniles, it must be because we should have different *normative* expectations. Young adolescents, the argument must run, cannot reasonably be expected to have a fully-fledged comprehension of the nature of other people's basic interests and how typical crimes affect those interests—because achieving this kind of understanding is a *developmental* process. It takes a greater degree of moral insight to appreciate how a house burglary affects someone's sense of security, than to know that it is against the law to enter and take his TV set. Developing that understanding calls both for cognitive skills and capacity for moral reasoning which develop over time—and

---

[13] D Husak and A von Hirsch, 'Culpability and Mistake of Law' in S Shute, J Gardner and J Horder (eds), *Action and Value in the Criminal Law* (Oxford, Oxford University Press, 1993) 163–65.

does so precisely during the period of adolescence. A 14- or 15-year-old has had less opportunity to develop the understanding of other people's interests that we reasonably may demand of an adult.

This brings us to the critical point of whether these cognitive arguments are chiefly descriptive or are normative in character. If descriptive, then claims to diminished culpability would depend on empirical evidence of reduced comprehension of consequences. But that degree of understanding varies greatly within a given age group: a clever 15-year-old will have a better grasp of such matters than a dull one—or even, than a dull adult. A descriptive approach could thus lead to diverse treatment of young persons of the same age, and call for trying to make elusive judgements about the degree of moral sophistication that a given adolescent has. It would also lead to the perverse consequence of punishing children with greater moral sophistication more severely—a difficulty that was apparent in the application of the (now-repealed) English rule of *doli incapax*.[14] Above all, a purely descriptive approach would fail to explain why a lesser appreciation of consequences *should* affect culpability.

Thus, the claim of reduced culpability is one that must have strong normative elements: it is not just that adolescents may in fact have a less full understanding of crimes' consequences. It is, rather, that this is all that we reasonably should demand of them, given the degree to which these qualities depend on experience, learning, and cognitive and volitional capacities that develop in adolescence over time. If children were to appear in the world fully fledged like Athena at her birth, our moral demands might well be more stringent. However, if this were the case, we would no longer be speaking of children.

In such a normative account, it is appropriate to employ age-based gradations. Because opportunities to develop cognitively and to gain experience are related to age, fuller comprehension may reasonably be expected of 17-year-old adolescents than of 14-year-old ones. A graded

---

[14] Under English criminal law until 1998, a child between the ages of 10 and 14 could be held criminally responsible only if the prosecution, in addition to establishing the elements of the crime, met a burden of showing that the child knew the conduct was wrong. In the Crime and Disorder Act 1998, s 34, this rule was eliminated. Instead of using the repeal of this rule to raise the age of criminal responsibility to 14, however, the Act *reduced* that age for all juvenile offenders to the astonishingly low level of 10 years.

scale thus should be utilised, in which there is a reduction in assessed crime-seriousness (and hence of sanction severity) based on age, and in which the reduction is greatest for those closest to the minimum age of criminal responsibility. What such a scale reflects are normative expectations, not actual patterns of development among individuals. It varies how much a particular 14-year-old, vis-à-vis a particular 17-year-old, actually grasps the typical harmful consequences of burglarising someone's home. But more may reasonably be expected of the 17-year-old, because he has had greater opportunity to grow towards adulthood.

11.2b Volitional Controls

Another aspect of culpability concerns *volitional controls*. Adolescents tend to be less able to postpone gratification, to control feelings of anger and aggression, and to resist peer pressures.[15] Self-restraint is more difficult to exercise when one is only 15.

With respect to this dimension, however, the relevant normative expectations become still more important: it must be asked why lesser self-control *should* be culpability-reducing. For adults, this characteristic would not ordinarily serve to mitigate fault. Were an adult criminal defendant to assert that his penalty should be reduced because of his deficient command of his impulses, we would ordinarily consider this to be a moral failing which did not render his conduct any less reprehensible. It is only if these deficiencies are based on significant mental or emotional disabilities that a claim for mitigation of punishment would be sustainable.[16] Why should the conclusion be otherwise for adolescents?

Self-control, as other aspects of moral development, is a *learned* capacity, and childhood and adolescence is the period during which it is learned. Angels might have self-discipline from the moment of their creation, but we do not and should not expect children to be born with similar capacities. It is through cognitive and emotional growth, interaction with others, and exposure to social norms that such capacities

---

[15] See Feld 1999, 309–13.
[16] Thus under Swedish sentencing law, it is deemed a mitigating factor that the defendant '... because of mental abnormality... had a reduced capacity to control his behaviour'; Swedish Penal Code, Ch 29, s 3: 2.

are gained; and this can be expected to occur not just in childhood, but also throughout adolescence. The adolescent who offends has had less time and opportunity to develop impulse-control and ability to resist the urgings of peers than the adult man or woman—which is why such factors properly bear on his degree of culpability. And as with the cognitive dimension discussed earlier, the expectations we should have should vary with age. As the adolescent approaches the age of adulthood, he should be expected to control himself better.

11.2c Youth 'Discount' or Individual Assessment?

If the foregoing culpability factors suggest reduced penalties for juveniles, should this involve categorical penalty reductions or individual determinations of culpability? The principle which the foregoing arguments support is one of categorical, age-related reductions. While actual appreciation of consequences varies greatly among youths of the same age, the degree of appreciation we should demand depends on age: we should expect more self-control from the 17-year-old than a 14-year-old, so that the 14-year-old's penalty should be less. Assessing culpability on the basis of individualised determinations of a youth's degree of moral development would be neither feasible nor desirable, for reasons already noted.

But even accepting this principle, the amount of sentence reduction will not be reducible to a simple formula. Numerical, age-related discounts from existing adult penalty levels would be unsatisfactory, because adult sentences for various offences should still represent a range of permissible dispositions, depending on the degree of harmfulness of the conduct and on the degree of culpability found in the particular case. Deciding upon the extent of age-related penalty reductions will have to involve qualitative judgement.

Aside from the categorical, age-related reductions, juveniles should also be entitled to certain individualised claims in mitigation of a kind that adults could also assert. A young offender may, for example, merit punishment below the level normally appropriate for his age, because he was only a peripheral actor in the offence, or was provoked.[17]

---

[17] Swedish Penal Code, Ch 29, s 3.

What requires further exploration is whether any special individualised mitigating claims should be recognised that hold for adolescents only. Even if we should not try usually to make individualised assessments of moral development, certain particular types of situations might be recognised where children have been confronted with unusually grave impediments to developing comprehension or self-control.[18] Taking such an approach would necessitate further reflection on what kinds of special circumstances should warrant such special mitigation.

11.3 PUNITIVE BITE

A second line of argument for penalty reduction that appears in the literature relates to 'punitive bite'. A given penalty is said to be more onerous when suffered by a youngster than by an adult. Young people, assertedly, are psychologically less resilient, and the punishments they suffer interfere more with their opportunities for education and personal development.[19]

Such claims, however, raise the question of what conception of punitive bite should be used. A possible perspective is a subjectivist one: that severity of a sanction depends on how unpleasant it is experienced as being.[20] Penalties thus are more onerous when applied to adolescents, simply because those persons will feel them more keenly. Such a subjectivist conception of severity would have troublesome implications, however. It would permit a high degree of variation among offenders of any given age. Some 15-year-olds are tough; others are tender, so that more stringent penalties might be visited on the tough ones, on the grounds that they suffer from them less. Measuring degrees of punitiveness by the sensitivities of particular offenders would also have worrisome social implications, to the extent that toughness and degree of inuredness to deprivation are related to social class.

The subjectivist view of penal severity strikes me, moreover, as being misconceived in principle. What makes punishments more or

---

[18] This might arguably be true, for example, for extraordinarily socially-deprived children.

[19] Zedner 1998, 173.

[20] For a subjectivist perspective on punitive bite, see AJ Kolber, 'The Subjective Experience of Punishment' (2009) *Columbia Law Review* 109, 182.

less severe is not sensations that vary greatly from person to person; it is rather, the extent to which those sanctions interfere with important interests that people have or should have. Interests are not merely subjective: they consist of resources over which persons have legitimate normative claims. The severity of imprisonment, for example should thus depend not just on it 'feeling bad', but on its interfering with such important resources as freedom of movement, privacy, personal autonomy in daily activities, and the right to choose one's associates (see, Chapter 6). It thus would be preferable to apply an interests-analysis to the assessment of punitive bite. Penalties should be ranked in severity according to the degree of importance of the interests affected, and the extent to which the penalty intrudes upon such interests. The importance of those interests may be gauged by the degree to which they affect an ordinary person's 'living standard'—that is, the resources and capabilities a person would ordinarily need to conduct a satisfactory life (see, Chapter 6, section 6.2).

How would this interests-analysis bear on gauging punitive bit for juveniles? Young people, it may be argued, have certain special interests; and punishment is more onerous for them because of its intrusion upon those interests. There are, first, certain *developmental interests*. Ordinarily, there are critical opportunities and experiences that need be provided to young persons between the ages of 14 and 18. A young person requires adequate schooling and learning opportunities; needs to be in a reasonably nurturing atmosphere and to have good adult role models; and needs to be able to develop ties with friends and associates whom he can trust. These are not mere preferences, but *interests*: a young person should have such resources in order to mature adequately. Punishments thus tend to be more onerous for adolescents because of the way they compromise these interests. This is most obviously true of imprisonment—which tends to stunt learning opportunities, provides a hostile rather than nurturing environment, offers few role models or destructive ones; and fosters attitudes of mistrust. If punishments are thus more onerous when undergone by juveniles, proportionality would require that they be scaled down.

A second type of interest relates to *capacity for self-esteem*. Given the censuring connotations of the criminal sanction, being punished scarcely promotes a person's self-esteem. It is not easy for anyone to undergo being punished without having his or her sense of self compromised; but the difficulty is greater for juveniles as they undergo adolescence. It is characteristic of adolescents that their self-esteem, their sense of self as worthwhile persons having the potential for a better future, tends to be more fragile (and can reasonably be expected to be more fragile) than that of adults. Again, this is a normative and not just a descriptive matter. Developing a robust conception of self, one that is resilient yet capable of evaluating and coping with the critical judgements of others, is a product of maturation and experience. It is thus appropriate to expect from juveniles a lesser degree of psychological resilience in the face of being punished than we should be able to demand of adults. Such normative judgements, again, are age-related. The younger the offender is, the less resilience can reasonably be demanded of him.

These developmental interests may point not only to a reduction in the severity of sanctions, but to differing criteria regarding *type* of sanction, even after controlling for severity. Those criteria may, for example, need to call for greater reliance on non-custodial penalties in preference even to short terms of imprisonment, given the disruptive effects of imprisonment on young persons' schooling, family life and socialties.[21]

11.4 A SPECIAL 'TOLERANCE' FOR JUVENILES?

So far, I have addressed the issues of culpability and punitive bite. Juveniles are to be punished less because (1) they are less culpable, and (2) punishments affect them more adversely. This still assumes, however, that the conventions linking penal severity with crime-seriousness are unchanged. Where the crimes (adjusting for culpability factors) have the same seriousness ratings, and where the penalties (adjusting for juveniles' greater vulnerability) have the same severity ratings, then juveniles and adults would receive equivalent punishments.

But might a further step be worth taking? Might not there be different conventions linking severity of punishment with seriousness of crimes for juveniles than for adults? This would constitute a stronger claim that young people deserve less: that there should be different and milder punishment conventions for juveniles, even after differences in culpability and in punitive 'bite' are taken into account. I believe such a

---

[21] For discussion of the possibility of interchanges between short prison terms and of non-custodial sentences, under a proportionalist model, see ch 8.

step would be desirable. The question then becomes, why so, and how can the adoption of a different punishment convention for juveniles be squared with notions of proportionality of sentence?

Youth, we know, is a time for experimentation; that is, for reducing reliance on adult guidance, for trying to live autonomously, for testing limits. As a result, it is a time for making mistakes, including those that harm others. Franklin Zimring likens this period of life to the period when a driver obtains a learners' permit: we know he will drive less well than an experienced driver, and hence is more likely to cause accidents; but we permit him to drive anyway (although, with specified restrictions) because it is only through doing so can he learn to become a competent driver.[22] Giving scope for this process of experimentation, Zimring argues, is particularly important in a modern society. There, we do not wish to train young persons to perform predetermined social roles, in the manner of traditional social systems. Instead, we wish to help them learn to act autonomously, and make their own life choices. That requires permitting adolescents to make their own choices, considering even the risks inevitably involved.

If these are the risks involved in permitting adolescents to experiment with acting autonomously, how do we deal with the harms that we know may result? The sensible response is one of cutting losses—of, in Zimring's words, 'keeping to a minimum the harm we inflict on [young offenders] when they have abused opportunities in ways that harm the community'.[23] Punishment policy for juveniles should be designed to 'preserve the life choices [even] for those who make serious mistakes'.[24] Again this is a gamble: that most of the juveniles who abuse such opportunities will, as they mature, learn how to live better autonomously—and should not be unduly burdened with the penal consequences of their earlier bad choices.

One way of reducing that burden is to adopt a punishment convention for juveniles which is less stringent than that for adults. Even after adjusting for differences in culpability and 'punitive bite', we should utilise milder punishment norms than would be applicable to adults. In punishing less, it is hoped that we will better preserve a young person's

---

[22] Zimring 1982 Ch 5.
[23] Ibid, 91.
[24] Ibid.

opportunities and prospects—and thus permit him or her to live freely as an adult, carrying fewer burdens from his or her earlier mistakes.

To what extent does this line of argument support diminished punishment levels for juveniles? There are several matters which need clarification. One concerns the consequences that can be expected of such a reduction. Can it be said that rates of juvenile crime will be lower if such a milder punishment scale is adopted? It might variously be said that, on one hand, milder sanctions will cause juveniles to self-identify less as criminals and hence come to offend less frequently; or, on the other hand, that such reduced sanctions may diminish marginal deterrent effects and hence cause youth crime to increase. Such potential effects cannot be gauged with even a modicum of confidence, however, given the limited state of knowledge of marginal deterrence and other crime-preventative effects.[25]

Any claim about the beneficial effects of this 'special tolerance' for youthful offenders should focus, instead, on how punishment affects the ordinary processes of growing up. Living autonomously involves not only making choices but being held accountable by others for those choices. Part of that accountability, a proportionalist sentencing rationale assumes, is undergoing penal censure for criminal wrongdoing. Punishment, however, also tends to interrupt the ordinary routines and developmental opportunities of growing up. A way of holding young people accountable but seeking to reduce potential damage to their life prospects is to adopt less stringent conventions for punishing adolescents.

This, however, does not yet take us to our desired conclusion. 'Cutting losses' is a *consequentialist* concern: it relates to the beneficial (or less injurious) consequences of punishing less. But a proportionalist sentencing rationale uses punishment criteria that are *retrospectively* oriented: it concerns the penal censure that is expressed through sanctions for misdeeds already committed. How, then, can the 'testing of limits' thesis be related to such retrospective criteria? We turn to this issue next.

In determining a proportionate sentence, the primary considerations are the seriousness of the criminal offence, and the degree of severity

---

[25] See above, ch 1, section 1.4; AE Bottoms and A von Hirsch, 'The Crime-Preventive Impact of Penal Sanctions' in P Cane and HM Kritzer (eds), *The Oxford Handbook of Empirical Legal Studies* (Oxford, Oxford University Press, 2010) Ch 4, 98–106.

of the punishment. These dimensions, as applied to juvenile offenders, have just been discussed. In certain contexts, however, there is an additional consideration, of what I have called a partial tolerance. The tolerance does not address offence-seriousness but rather, how much penal censure should attach to conduct of a given degree of seriousness. The idea of the partial tolerance is that, in certain situations, we should entertain a certain degree of sympathy for the predicament of those punished—and hence utilise more forgiving punishment standards.

I have applied this notion of a partial tolerance in a different context, namely, in order to argue for a discount in the punishments of (adult) first offenders (Chapter 7). My suggested first-offender discount is also not based on a claim of reduced culpability; it applies to the first offender who appears to be fully culpable—for example, quite aware of the wrongfulness of his conduct. The essence of the claim is that even if the first offence reflects no less culpability, it should be judged by less stringent standards.

The partial tolerance for the first offender, I have suggested, should rest on the notion of a *lapse*.[26] A transgression (even of penal statutes) is to be judged less stringently when it occurs against a background of prior compliance. The idea is that even an ordinarily well-behaved person may have his moral inhibitions fail in a moment of willfulness or weakness. Such a lapse reflects a kind of human frailty for which some sympathy should be shown.

Should a comparable tolerance thesis be applied to juveniles, to justify a milder punishment convention? I think it can—although its particulars would need to operate differently. The notion of adolescence as a time of testing, sketched above, provides good reason for granting a partial tolerance. Why does it do so? The point to emphasise is not just that adolescents are more liable to overstep legal limits. It is, rather, that the situation in which they are placed, of being encouraged to begin making autonomous choices, encourages experimentation on their part and hence risks the overstepping of bounds. If young persons are supposed to 'try out' making their own decisions, notwithstanding harmful choices that might ensue, then there should be some special sympathy for failures, and those should be judged by a less stringent standard.

A few features of this argument are worth noting. First, it is different to the claim made earlier, that juvenile offenders are less culpable. This

---

[26] See ch 7.

tolerance argument is not reducible to claims about lesser understanding of consequences, and less adequate impulse control. It is, rather, that young persons, when given the opportunity of more autonomous living, might well make the wrong choices—including wrongs for which they know the harmful consequences full well, and which they could well have avoided making. Learning to make choices carries with it the risk of making *bad* choices.

Second, the tolerance should *generally* be available to youthful offenders. Any youth, in virtue of the status of adolescence, faces the predicaments involved in learning to live in freedom, and thus should be entitled to a degree of sympathy for transgressing the limits.

Third and critically, the tolerance is *temporary*. It should be greatest in early adolescence, and gradually diminish with the approach of the age of majority. This comports with the underlying rationale—that adolescence is a time for learning to live in freedom. When adulthood is reached, the person will already have had the opportunity to test limits, and should be answerable as an adult.

How does this account bear upon Zimring's thesis about youth as a time for testing? His arguments are, as noted above, consequentialist: that less harm to juveniles will be done if penalties are scaled down. What we need, in order to justify penalty reduction under a proportionalist sentencing rationale, is a retrospectively-oriented reason—and that (I think) is supplied by the tolerance argument. Scaling down punishments is not just a matter of avoiding undesirable consequences in future; but that it is morally appropriate to judge juveniles by a less stringent standard in view of the predicaments they face learning how to live autonomously.

For further reading:

Duff, RA (2002) 'Punishing the Young' in I Weijers and RA Duff (eds), *Punishing Juveniles: Principle and Critique* (Oxford, Hart Publishing).

Feld, Barry C (2012) 'Adolescent Criminal Responsibility, Proportionality, and Sentencing Policy' *Law & Inequality* 31, 263.

Feld, Barry (1999) *Bad Kids: Race and the Transformation of the Juvenile Court* (New York, Oxford University Press).

Scott, Elizabeth S and L Steinberg (2002) 'Blaming Youth' *Texas Law Review* 81, 799

Shust, Kelsey B (2014) 'Extending Sentencing Mitigation for Deserving Young Adults' *Journal of Criminal Law & Criminology* 104, 667.

Appendix

The Desert Model's Evolution—
A Brief Chronology

TO PROVIDE A compact account of the desert model, this book has presented it as a unified theory. That mode of presentation is intended to make the model and its justifying arguments more readily comprehensible; and to elucidate the relationship among its various elements.

The model, however, was not developed at a single time, nor by a single author. Rather, it has evolved over an extended period, with various themes being added at different times, by various contributors. Let me sketch some milestones in this course of evolution.

1. *Doing Justice and its Genesis.* The work *Doing Justice*[1] was the report of the Committee for the Study of Incarceration, a group mainly comprised of criminologists, legal scholars, and other interested theorists.[2] The group was chaired by former US Senator Charles E Goodell. I had been Senator Goodell's principal legislative assistant during his previous tenure in the US Senate, and was designated as the Committee's executive director and project chief of staff. It was decided at the outset that the Committee should undertake a fundamental reconsideration of the conceptual and normative basis for sentencing policy.

In the decades before the Committee began its work in the early 1970s, there existed a prevailing conception of sentencing, embodied in such documents as the American Law Institute's *Model*

---

[1] A von Hirsch, *Doing Justice: The Choice of Punishments* (New York, Hill and Wang, 1976; reprinted 1986 (Boston, Northeastern University Press)); see ch 1.

[2] The Committee's members were: Former US Senator Charles E Goodell (chair); Marshall Cohen; Samuel du Bois Cook; Alan M Dershowitz; Willard Gaylin; Erving Goffman; Joseph Goldstein; Jorge Lara-Braud; Victor Marrero; Eleanor Holmes Norton; David J Rothman; Simon Rottenberg; Herman Schwarz; Stanton Wheeler; and Leslie T Wilkins.

Penal Code (1962).[3] This perspective made individual crime prevention the primary basis of sentencing. Emphasis was placed upon the
offender's need for rehabilitation; and upon his estimated likelihood of
returning to crime. The sentencing judge's task was to suit the disposition to the offender's need for treatment and his risk of recidivism. To
achieve these aims, judges were supposed to be granted wide discretion
to fashion the sentence to the needs of the individual offender.

By the time the Committee commenced its deliberations in early
1972, there were signs of disenchantment with this treatment-and-
prediction paradigm. Evidence was accumulating that offender rehabilitation programmes, when carefully evaluated, yielded disappointing
results in reducing offenders rates of returning to crime. Similarly, predictions of offenders' likelihood of recidivism showed a disturbingly
high incidence of 'false positives'—that is, offenders being mistakenly
classified as potential law-breakers.

The Committee's initial discussions confirmed such growing scepticism about the then prevailing sentencing ethos.[4] The group also
quickly came to favour explicit constraints on sentencing and paroling
discretion, through rules or guiding principles which criminal justice
decision-makers would be called upon to take into account in their
decisions concerning individual cases.

The group then turned its attention to the aim of retribution—or,
as it came to be called in our deliberations, desert. Influential in our
discussions was a 1965 article by the American legal philosopher Joel
Feinberg, entitled, 'The Expressive Function of Punishment'.[5] He

---

[3] American Law Institute 1962.

[4] In 1992, the first year of the Committee's deliberations, the group approved
a paper of mine that was highly critical of prediction-based sentencing schemes:
A von Hirsch (1972) 'Prediction of Criminal Conduct and Preventive Confinement
of Convicted Persons' (1972) *Buffalo Law Review* 21, 717.

[5] This article was reprinted in J Feinberg, *Doing and Deserving* (Princeton, Princeton University Press, 1970) Ch 5. Also influential in the Committee's deliberations
was an earlier article on the punishment's censuring implications by the Harvard
legal scholar Henry M Hart, see HM Hart Jr 'The Aims of the Criminal Law'
(1958) *Law & Contemporary Problems* 23, 401. A desert-based account of sentencing, by the Australian philosopher John Kleinig, also appeared in 1973 during the
Committee's deliberations. That account however did not rely on a censure-based
conception of desert.

asserted that punishment has, as an essential feature, disapprobation or censure. Punishing someone for given conduct, he argued, implies that the conduct is wrongful—and that the actor may justifiably be blamed or censured for committing it.

The introduction of this theme of punishment's censuring character suggested giving desert considerations a substantially increased role. If an offender's punishment involves disapprobation or censure of his conduct, then the conduct's degree of blameworthiness should play a substantially increased role in the determination of his sentence.

The question remained for the Committee, however, of how central a place such considerations of blameworthiness should be accorded. In the Committee's discussions, I came to argue that desert should become the preeminent consideration—and I drafted a series of discussion papers so proposing. This somewhat radical view, however, did not achieve consensus within the Committee. However, no compromise view combining desert and traditional sentencing perspectives suggested itself to the group as preferable. It was felt, nevertheless, that a desert conception should play a substantial role in sentencing decisions and that this was of sufficient importance to be introduced by the Committee into public debate.

The Committee's agreed-upon solution was to publish my desert-oriented draft as the Committee's report, but with myself named as its principal author. Individual members of the Committee were then asked whether they supported the report's recommendations 'on balance'—but with space allotted for members' individual views. On this basis, all the members signed the report, but several of them added their own statements. The expressed views of individual members ranged from substantial concurrence to near-complete dissensus. Of particular interest was the book's introduction by the historian David J Rothman and the psychoanalyst Willard Gaylin, which gave the report's conclusions qualified support, but expressed greater sympathy for rehabilitative aspirations than the text conveyed. The book made its appearance in 1976, and attracted widespread interest—indeed, much more than the Committee members or I had expected.

2. *The 'Why Punish at All?' Question.* This question is addressed in Chapter 3 of the present volume. It concerns a question that goes beyond sentencing theory—namely, why the institution of the penal system should exist at all. *Doing Justice* had addressed this issue by seeking to combine the censure perspective with the so-called

'benefits-and-burdens' theory.[6] The deficiencies of this latter view were pointed out to me during my subsequent visits to Uppsala University by Swedish colleagues, most notably Professor Nils Jareborg. He also suggested (and convinced me) that the criminal sanction had, in addition to its censuring role, an essential preventive element of supplying a disincentive to criminal behaviour. I developed a revised account reflecting that view in a Swedish-language article—and subsequently in an English version published in 1983.[7] Further reflection led to a more fully worked-out formulation of that account, which appeared in my 1993 volume, *Censure and Sanctions*[8]—and which Chapter 3 of the present volume reflects.

3. *Cardinal vs Ordinal Proportionality*. This distinction was developed a few years after the publication of *Doing Justice*. It responded to an important challenge to the desert model made by the noted University of Chicago criminologist, Norval Morris.[9] His contention was that desert requirements were indeterminate: that whereas we have some sense of when punishments appear to be grossly excessive or manifestly insufficient, we lack the ability to discern with any degree of definiteness how much punishment any given type of crime should deserve. Desert, he asserted, thus can only fix broad outer limits, within which penalties should be fixed on utilitarian grounds of crime prevention. My response was to suggest the distinction between ordinal and cardinal proportionality, described in Chapter 5. This response was developed after extensive discussions with Morris' collaborator, Michael Tonry, and was first sketched in a 1983 article of mine.[10] The distinction was then developed more fully in my next book on desert

---

[6] This theory is described and criticised in ch 3, text at nn 5–6.

[7] A von Hirsch, 'Neoclassicism, Proportionality, and the Rationale for Punishment: Thoughts on the Scandinavian Debate' (1983) *Crime & Delinquency* 29, 52.

[8] A von Hirsch, *Censure and Sanctions* (Oxford, Oxford University Press, 1993) Ch 2; see also A von Hirsch and A Ashworth, *Proportionate Sentencing: Exploring the Principles* (Oxford, Oxford University Press, 2005) Ch 2.

[9] See N Morris, *Punishment, Desert, and Rehabilitation* (Washington DC, US Government Printing Office, 1976); N Morris, *Madness and the Criminal Law* (Chicago, Chicago University Press, 1982) Ch 5.

[10] A von Hirsch, 'Recent Trends in American Criminal Sentencing Theory' (1983) *Maryland Law Review* 42, 6.

theory, *Past or Future Crimes* (1985),[11] and is addressed in Chapter 5 of this book.

4. *Gauging Seriousness of Crime*. This topic was addressed briefly in *Doing Justice*, but without reaching definite conclusions.[12] On a visit to Sweden in 1986 and on subsequent visits, Nils Jareborg and I discussed the topic extensively, and came to believe that crime-seriousness had something to do with how much various kinds of criminal conduct affect people's quality of life. However, I still lacked a fuller account of what conception of life-quality should be utilised. A conversation with John Kleinig, an early advocate of desert theory, provided the clue: he called our attention to the Harvard philosopher and economist Amartya Sen's book, *The Standard of Living* (1987).[13] As described in Chapter 6, we used Sen's notion of the living-standard as the basis for assessing crime-seriousness and punishment-severity, in a jointly-authored article (1991)[14] and also in my subsequently published volume, *Censure and Sanctions* (1993).[15] The topic is addressed in this volume in Chapter 6.

5. *The Role of Previous Convictions*. Ordinary people have a sense that an offender's previous convictions alter how much he deserves, but the issue becomes puzzling when one asks why. In *Doing Justice*, I attempted an explanation: that reoffending after previous convictions alters the offender's culpability in committing the new offence. That explanation, however, soon seemed to me unsatisfactory, and several other colleagues also raised their doubts.

I began to develop my present theory concerning a 'tolerance', beginning with a 1981 article;[16] and gradually expanded this through

---

[11] A von Hirsch, *Past or Future Crimes: Deservedness and Dangerousness in the Sentencing of Criminals* (New Brunswick, New Jersey, Rutgers University Press, 1985; United Kingdom edn 1986 (Manchester, Manchester University Press)) Ch 4.

[12] von Hirsch 1976, Ch 9.

[13] A Sen, *The Standard of Living* (Cambridge, Cambridge University Press, 1987).

[14] A von Hirsch and N Jareborg, 'Gauging Criminal Harm: A Living-Standard Analysis' (1991) *Oxford Journal of Legal Studies* 11, 1.

[15] von Hirsch 1993, Ch 4.

[16] A von Hirsch, 'Desert and Previous Convictions in Sentencing' (1981) *Minnesota Law Review* 65, 591.

the next decades, resulting in a full account in a 2010 essay[17]—which my treatment of the subject in Chapter 7 reflects.

6. *Non-Custodial Penalties.* A desert-based sentencing scheme needs to deal also with non-custodial penalties. Once prison sanctions' severity is recognised, it is clear that they are appropriate chiefly for serious crimes—thus calling for less onerous non-custodial sanctions for offences of intermediate and lesser seriousness. The traditional non-custodial penalty, probation, seemed too indeterminate and too much linked with rehabilitation to serve well in this role. The desert model thus needs to devise an adequate array of intermediate and lesser sanctions not involving imprisonment, that would be capable of being graded according to crime seriousness, as the desert model requires. Thus, it is not surprising that, beginning in the 1980s, penologists turned their attention to the subject of non-custodial penalties.

I had not given sufficient thought to this subject until contacted by an English colleague, Martin Wasik, who recognised sooner than I that an account of desert-based non-custodial penalties was urgently needed. We met in the mid-80s, and spent some time devising such a scheme—which appeared in a jointly-authored 1988 law review article.[18] This Wasik–von Hirsch model was then discussed in a subsequent book of mine on desert theory,[19] and is addressed here in Chapter 8.

7. *Juvenile Offenders.* Although the question of the applicability of the desert model to juvenile justice occasionally occurred to me, I did not begin to think in earnest about it until I read a 1998 article on the

---

[17] A von Hirsch, 'Proportionality and the Progressive Loss of Mitigation: Some Further Reflections' in A von Hirsch and JV Roberts (eds), *Previous Convictions at Sentencing: Theoretical and Applied Perspectives* (Oxford, Hart Publishing, 2010) Ch 1.

[18] M Wasik and A von Hirsch, 'Non-Custodial Penalties and the Principles of Desert' (1988) *Criminal Law Review* 555. Shortly thereafter, Norvel Morris and Michael Tonry published their influential volume on scaling non-custodial penalties entitled, *Between Prison and Probation*, based on their 'limiting retributivism' conception of sentencing discussed in Chapter 10; see N Morris and M Tonry, *Between Prison and Probation: Intermediate Punishments in a Rational Sentencing System* (New York, Oxford University Press, 1990).

[19] von Hirsch 1993, Ch 7.

subject by my Oxford colleague Lucia Zedner.[20] I then also turned to the writings on juvenile justice of two American colleagues, Franklin Zimring and Barry Feld. My own article suggesting how a desert-based conception should apply to juvenile justice appeared in 2001,[21] and is the basis of Chapter 11 of this volume.

[20] L Zedner, 'Sentencing Young Offenders' in A Ashworth and M Wasik (eds), *Fundamentals of Sentencing Theory* (Oxford, Oxford University Press, 1998) Ch 7.

[21] A von Hirsch, 'Proportionate Sentencing for Juveniles: How Different than for Adults?' (2001) *Punishment & Society* 3, 221.

Bibliography

American Friends Service Committee (1972) *Struggle for Justice* (New York, Hill and Wang).

American Law Institute (1962) *Model Penal Code* (Philadelphia, American Law Institute).

Andenaes, Johannes (1982) *Punishment and Deterrence* (Ann Arbor, Michigan, University of Michigan Press).

—— (1988) 'Nyklassicisme, Proporsjonalitet og Prevensjon' *Nordisk Tidsskrift for Kriminalvidenskab* 75, 41.

Apel, Robert (2013) 'Sanctions, Perceptions, and Crime: Implications for Criminal Deterrence' *Journal of Quantitative Criminology* 29, 67.

Armstrong, KG (1961) 'The Retributivist Hits Back' *Mind* 70, 471.

Ashworth, Andrew (1983) *Sentencing and Penal Policy* (London, Heinemanns).

—— (1989) 'Criminal Justice and Deserved Sentences' *Criminal Law Review* 340.

—— (2010) 'Sentencing Guidelines and the Sentencing Council' *Criminal Law Review* 389.

—— (2015) *Sentencing and Criminal Justice*, 6th edn (Cambridge, Cambridge University Press).

Ashworth, A and JV Roberts (eds) (2013) *Sentencing Guidelines: Exploring the English Model* (Oxford, Oxford University Press).

Ashworth, A and L Zedner (2014) *Preventive Justice* (New York, Oxford University Press).

Asp, Peter and A von Hirsch (1999) 'Straffvärde' *Svensk Juristtidning* 151.

Ball, C, K McCormac, and N Stone (1995) *Young Offenders: Law, Policy and Practice* (London, Sweet & Maxwell).

Beccaria, Cesare (1963) *Of Crimes and Punishments*. Translated by Henry Paolucci (Indianapolis, Bobbs-Merrill (Original 1764)).

Bentham, Jeremy (1982) *An Introduction to the Principles of Morals and Legislation* (edited by JH Byrne and HLA Hart) (London, Methuen (Original 1789)).

Bierschbach, RA (2012) 'Proportionality and Parole' *University of Pennsylvania Law Review* 160, 1745.

Bottoms, AE (1989) 'The Concept of Intermediate Sanctions and its Relevance for the Probation Service' in E Shaw and K Haines (eds), *The Criminal Justice System: A Central Role for the Probation Service* (Cambridge, Institute of Criminology).

—— (1998) 'Five Puzzles in von Hirsch's Theory' in A Ashworth and M Wasik (eds), *Fundamentals of Sentencing Theory: Essays in Honour of Andrew von Hirsch* (Oxford, Oxford University Press) Ch 3.

Bottoms, AE and R Brownsword (1983) 'Dangerousness and Rights' in JW Hinton (ed), *Dangerousness: Problems of Assessment and Prediction* (London, George Allen & Unwin).

Bottoms, AE and A von Hirsch (2010) 'The Crime-Preventive Impact of Penal Sanctions' in P Cane and HM Kritzer (eds), *The Oxford Handbook of Empirical Legal Studies* (Oxford, Oxford University Press) Ch 4.

Braithwaite, J and P Pettit (1990) *Not Just Deserts: A Republican Theory of Justice.* (Oxford, Oxford University Press).

Brottsförebyggande Rådet (1977) *Nytt Strafsystem: Idéer och Förslag* (Stockholm, Brottsförebyggande Rådet).

Bruce, Jacobs and A Piquero (2013) 'Boundary-Crossing in Perceptual Deterrence' *International Journal of Offender Therapy and Comparative Criminology* 57, 792.

Bruns, HJ (1985) *Das Recht der Strafzumessung*, 2nd edn (Cologne, Carl Heymanns Verlag).

Cameron, Iain (1998) *An Introduction to the European Convention on Human Rights*, 3rd edn (Uppsala, Iustus).

Christie, N (2002) *Crime Control as Industry: Towards Gulags, Western Style*, 3rd edn (London, Routledge).

Cullen, Francis T and KE Gilbert (2012) *Reaffirming Rehabilitation.* 2nd edn (London, Routledge).

Davis, Michael (1983) 'How to Make the Punishment Fit the Crime' *Ethics* 93, 726.

Dolinko, David (1992) 'Three Mistakes about Retributivism' *University of Chicago Law Review* 39, 1623.

Doob, Anthony (1995) 'The United States Sentencing Commission Guidelines' In C Clarkson and R Morgan (eds), *The Politics of Sentencing Reform* (Oxford, Oxford University Press) Ch 6.

Duff, RA (1986) *Trials and Punishments* (Cambridge, Cambridge University Press).

—— (2001) *Punishment, Communication, and Community* (New York, Oxford University Press).

—— (2002) 'Punishing the Young' in I Weijers and RA Duff (eds), *Punishing Juveniles: Principle and Critique* (Oxford, Hart Publishing) Ch 6.

Dworkin, Ronald (1977), *Taking Rights Seriously* (Cambridge, Massachusetts, Harvard University Press).

Fängelsestraffkommittén (1986) *Påföljd för Brott* (Stockholm, Stadens Offentlige Utredingar).

Federal Sentencing Guidelines Manual (2011) Washington DC, US Sentencing Commission, available at www.ussc.gov/guidelines-manual/2011/2011-federal-sentencing-guidelines-manual.

Feinberg, Joel (1970) *Doing and Deserving* (Princeton, Princeton University Press).

Feld, Barry (1999) *Bad Kids: Race and the Transformation of the Juvenile Court* (New York, Oxford University Press).

—— (2012) 'Adolescent Criminal Responsibility, Proportionality, and Sentencing Policy' *Law and Inequality* 31, 263.

—— (2013) 'Youth Discount: Old Enough to Do the Crime, Too Young to Do the Time' *Ohio State Journal of Criminal Law* 11, 107.

Feld, Barry C and DM Bishop (eds) (2012) *The Oxford Handbook of Juvenile Crime and Juvenile Justice* (New York, Oxford University Press).

Finnis, John (1980) *Natural Law and Natural Rights* (Oxford, Oxford University Press).

Fletcher, George (1978) *Rethinking Criminal Law* (Boston, Little-Brown).

—— (1982) 'The Recidivist Premium' *Criminal Justice Ethics* 1(2) 54.

Frase, Richard S (2004) 'Excessive Prison Sentences, Punishment Goals, and the Eighth Amendment: Proportionality Relative to What?' *Minnesota Law Review* 89, 571.

—— (2013) *Just Sentencing: Principles and Procedures for a Workable System* (New York, Oxford University Press).

Friedman, D and W Sjöström (1993) 'Hanged for a Sheep—the Economics of Marginal Deterrence' *Journal of Legal Studies* 22, 345.

Frisch, Wolfgang (1998) 'Schwächen und berechtigte Aspekte der Theorie der positiven Generalprävention' in B Schünemann, A von Hirsch and N Jareborg (eds), *Positive Generalprävention* (Heidelberg, CF Müller).

Gardner, Martin (1976) 'The Renaissance of Retribution: In Examination of "Doing Justice"' *Wisconsin Law Review* 781.

Greenfield, Victoria A and Letizia Paoli (2013) 'A Framework to Assess the Harms of Crimes' *British Journal of Criminology* 53, 864.

Greenwood, Peter W (1982) *Selective Incapacitation* (Santa Monica, California, RAND Corporation).

Haist, Matthew (2009) 'Deterrence in a Sea of Just Deserts: Are Utilitarian Goals Achievable in a World of Limiting Retributivism?' *Journal of Criminal Law & Criminology* 99, 789.

Hart, HM Jr (1958) 'The Aims of the Criminal Law' *Law & Contemporary Problems* 23, 401.

Heckscher, Sten et al (eds) (1980) *Straff och rättfärdighet: Ny nordisk debatt* (Stockolm, Norstedts).

Hill, M, A Lockyer and F Stone (eds) (2007) *Youth Justice and Child Protection* (London, Jessica Kingsley).

Hörnle, Tatjana (1999) *Tatproportionale Strafzumessung* (Berlin, Duncker und Humblot).

Hudson, Barbara (1987) Justice through Punishment: A Critique of the 'Justice' Model of Corrections (London, St Martins).

—— (1998) 'Doing Justice to Difference' in A Ashworth and M Wasik (eds), *Fundamentals of Sentencing Theory: Essays in Honour of Andrew von Hirsch* (Oxford, Oxford University Press) Ch 9.

Husak, Douglas (2011) 'Retributivism, Propotionality, and the Challenge of the Drug Court Movement' in M Tonry (ed), *Retributivism Has a Past; Has it a Future?* (New York, Oxford University Press) Ch 11.

Husak, Douglas and A von Hirsch (1993) 'Culpability and Mistake of Law' in S Shute, J Gardner and J Horder (eds) *Action and Value in the Criminal Law* (Oxford, Oxford University Press).

Jareborg, Nils (1988) *Essays in Criminal Law* (Uppsala, Iustus).

—— (1992) 'Ideology and Crime: Basic Conceptions of Crime and Their Implications' in R Lahti and K Nuotio (eds), *Criminal Law in Transition: Finnish and Comparative Perspectives* (Helsinki, Finnish Lawyers' Publishing Co).

—— (1995) 'The Swedish Sentencing Reform' in C Clarkson and R Morgan (eds), *The Politics of Sentencing Reform* (Oxford, Oxford University Press).

Kahan, Dan M (1996), 'What Do Alternative Sanctions Mean?' *University of Chicago Law Review* 63, 591.

Kleinig, John (1973) *Punishment and Desert* (The Hague, Nijhoff).

—— (1991) 'Punishment and Moral Seriousness' *Israel Law Review* 25, 401.

—— (2011) 'What Does Wrongdoing Deserve?' in M Tonry (ed), *Retributivism Has a Past. Has It a Future?* (New York, Oxford University Press) Ch 3.

Kolber, Adam J (2009) 'The Subjective Experience of Punishment' *Columbia Law Review* 109, 182.

Lacey, Nicola (2008) *The Prisoner's Dilemma: Political Economy and Punishment in Contemporary Democracies* (Cambridge, Cambridge University Press).

Lacey, Nicola and H Pickard (2015) 'The Chimera of Proportionality: Institutionalising Limits on Punishment in Contemporary Social and Political Systems' *Modern Law Review* 78, 216.

Lappi-Seppälä, Tapio (1998) *Regulating the Prison Population: Experiences from a Long-Term Policy in Finland* (Helsinki, National Research Institute of Legal Policy).

—— (2007) 'Penal Policy in Scandinavia' in M Tonry (ed), *Crime, Punishment, and Politics in a Comparative Perspective. Crime and Justice* (Chicago, Chicago University Press) Vol 36.

Laub, JH and RJ Sampson (2001) 'Understanding Desistance from Crime' in M Tonry (ed), *Crime and Justice: A Review of Research* (Chicago, Chicago University Press) Vol 28.

Lee, Youngjae (2005) 'The Constitutional Right Against Excessive Punishment' *Virginia Law Review* 91, 677.

—— (2010) 'Repeat Offenders and the Question of Desert' in JV Roberts and A von Hirsch (eds), *Previous Convictions at Sentencing* (Oxford, Hart Publishing) Ch 4.

Lippke, Richard L (2007) *Rethinking Imprisonment* (New York, Oxford University Press).

Lovegrove, Austin (2001) 'Sanctions and Severity: To the Demise of von Hirsch & Wasik's Sanction Hierarchy' *Howard Journal of Criminal Justice* 40, 126.

Marcus, Michael (2007) 'Limiting Retributivism: Revisions to Model Penal Code Sentencing Provisions' *Whittier Law Review* 29, 295.

Martinson, R (1974) 'What Works?—Questions and Answers about Prison Reform' *Public Interest* 35, 25.

Matravers, Matt (2011) 'Is Twenty-First Century Punishment Post-Desert?' In M Tonry (ed), *Retributivism Has a Past: Has It a Future?* (New York, Oxford University Press) Ch 2.

Moore, Michael (1997) *Placing Blame: A General Theory of Criminal Law* (Oxford, Clarendon Press).

Morris, Herbert (1968) 'Persons and Punishments' *Monist* 52, 475.

Morris, Norval (1976), *Punishment, Desert, and Rehabilitation* (Washington, DC, US Government Printing Office).

—— (1982) *Madness and the Criminal Law* (Chicago, Chicago University Press).

Morris, Norval and M Tonry (1990) *Between Prison and Probation: Intermediate Punishments in a Rational Sentencing System* (New York, Oxford University Press).

National Academy of Sciences, Panel on Research on Criminal Careers (1986) *Criminal Careers and 'Career Criminals'* (edited by A Blumstein, J Cohen, J Roth and C Visher) (Washington DC, National Academies of Sciences Press) Vol 1.

National Council of Crime and Delinquency (1963) Council of Judges 'Model Sentencing Act' *Crime and Delinquency* 9, 337.

Narayan, Uma (1993) 'Adequate Responses and Preventive Benefits: Justifying Censure and Hard Treatment in Legal Punishment' *Oxford Journal of Legal Studies* 13, 166.

Padfield, N (2011) 'Time to Bury the Custody "Threshold"?' *Criminal Law Review* 8, 593.

Perez, MB and R Argueta (2014) 'Selective Incapacitation' in J Albanese (ed), *The Encyclopedia of Criminology and Criminal Justice* (New Jersey, Wiley).

Petersilia, J, P Greenwood and M Lavin (1977) *Criminal Careers of Habitual Felons.* (Santa Monica, California, RAND Corporation).

Piquero, Alex R, DP Farrington and A Blumstein (2003), 'The Criminal Career Paradigm' in M Tonry (ed). *Crime and Justice: A Review of Research* (Chicago, Chicago University Press) Vol 30, 359.

Reiman, Jeffrey and S Headlee (1981) 'Marxism and Criminal Justice Policy' *Crime & Delinquency* 27, 24.

Reitz, Kevin R (2006) 'Don't Blame Determinacy: US Incarceration Growth Has Been Driven by Other Forces' *Texas Law Review* 84, 1787.

Rex, Sue (2013) *Reforming Community Penalties* (London, Routledge).

Rich, Michael L (2013) 'Limits on the Perfect Preventive State' *Connecticut Law Review* 46, 883.

Roberts, Julian V (2010), 'First Offender Sentencing Discounts: Exploring the Justifications' in JV Roberts and A von Hirsch (eds), *Previous Convictions at Sentencing* (Oxford, Hart Publishing) Ch 2.

Roberts, Julian V and O Gazal-Ayal (2013) 'Statutory Sentencing Reform in Israel: Exploring the Sentencing Law of 2012' *Israel Law Review* 46, 455.

Robinson, Paul H (1987) 'Hybrid Principles for the Distribution of Criminal Sanctions' *Northwestern Law Review* 82, 19.

Robinson, Paul H and R Kurzban (2006) 'Concordance and Conflict in Intuitions of Justice' *Minnesota Law Review* 91, 1829.

Roebuck, Greg and D Wood (2011) 'A Retributive Argument Against Punishment' *Criminal Law & Philosophy* 5, 73.

Roxin, Claus (1979) 'Zur jüngsten Diskussion über Schuld, Prävention und Verantwortlichkeit im Strafrecht' in A Kaufmann et al (eds), *Festschrift für Paul Bockelmann* (München, CH Beck).

—— (2014) 'Prevention, Censure and Responsibility: The Recent Debate on the Purposes of Punishment' in AP Simester, A Du Bois-Pedain and U Neumann (eds), *Liberal Criminal Theory: Essays for Andreas von Hirsch* (Oxford, Hart Publishing) Ch 2.

Ryberg, Jesper (2007) *The Ethics of Proportionate Punishment: A Critical Investigation* (Dordrecht, Kluwer Academic Publishers).

Schumann, Karl F (1998) 'Empirische Beweisbarkeit der Grundannahmen von positiver Generalprävention' in B Schünemann, A von Hirsch and N Jareborg (eds), *Positive Generalprävention* (Heidelberg, CF Müller).

Schünemann, Bernd, A von Hirsch and N Jareborg (1998) *Positive Generalprävention: Kritische Perspektiven in deutsch-englischem Dialog* (Heidelberg, CF Müller).

Scott, Elizabeth S and L Steinberg (2002) 'Blaming Youth' *Texas Law Review* 81, 799.

Sebba, Leslie and G Nathan (1984), 'Further Exploration of the Scaling of Penalties' *British Journal of Criminology* 24, 221.

Sellin, Thorsten and M Wolfgang (1964) *The Measurement of Delinquency* (New York, John Wiley).

Sen, Amartya (1987) *The Standard of Living* (Cambridge, Cambridge University Press).

—— (2009) *The Idea of Justice* (Cambridge, Massachusetts, Harvard University Press).

Sentencing Guidelines Council (England and Wales) (2004) *Overarching Principles: Seriousness* (London, Sentencing Guidelines Council).

—— (2009). *Overarching Principles—Sentencing Youths* (London, Sentencing Guidelines Council).

Simester, AP and A von Hirsch (2011) *Crimes, Harms, and Wrongs. On the Principles of Criminalisation* (Oxford, Hart Publishing).

Slobogin, C (2011) 'Prevention as the Primary Goal of Sentencing: The Modern Case for Interdeterminate Dispositions in Criminal Cases' *San Diego Law Review* 48, 1127.

Staihar, Jim (2015) 'Proportionality and Punishment' *Iowa Law Review* 100, 1209–32.

Steiker, C (2013) 'Proportionality as a Limit on Preventive Justice: Promises and Pitfalls' in A Ashworth, L Zedner and P Toulmin (eds), *Prevention and the Limits of the Criminal Law* (Oxford, Oxford University Press).

Stigler, George (1970) 'The Optimum Enforcement of Laws' *Journal of Political Economy* 78, 526.

Strawson, Peter (1974) *Freedom and Resentment and Other Essays* (London, Methuen) Ch 1.

Streng, Franz (2012) *Strafrechtliche Sanktionen: Die Strafzumessung und ihre Grundlagen*, 3rd edn (Stuttgart, Kohlhammer).

Stylianou, Stelios (2003) 'Measuring Crime Seriousness Perceptions: What Have We Learned and What Else Do We Want to Know' *Journal of Criminal Justice* 31, 37.

Tonry, Michael (2004). *Punishment and Politics: Evidence and Emulation in the Making of English Crime Control Policy* (Cullompton, Willan Publishing).

UK Government White Paper (1990) *Crime, Justice and Protecting the Public* (London, HMSO).

US Sentencing Commission (1987) *Federal Sentencing Guidelines Manual* (Washington DC, US Sentencing Commission).

van den Haag (1987) 'Punishment: Desert and Control' *Michigan Law Review* 85, 1250.

von Hirsch, A (1972) 'Prediction of Criminal Conduct and Preventive Confinement of Convicted Persons' *Buffalo Law Review* 21, 717.

—— (1976) *Doing Justice: The Choice of Punishments* (New York, Hill and Wang; Reprinted 1986 (Boston, Northeastern University Press)).

—— (1981) 'Desert and Previous Convictions in Sentencing' *Minnesota Law Review* 65, 591.

—— (1983) 'Neoclassicism, Proportionality, and the Rationale for Punishment: Thoughts on the Scandinavian Debate' *Crime & Delinquency* 29, 52.

—— (1983) 'Recent Trends in American Criminal Sentencing Theory' *Maryland Law Review* 42, 6.

—— (1985) *Past or Future Crimes: Deservedness and Dangerousness in the Sentencing of Criminals* (New Brunswick, New Jersey, Rutgers University Press; United Kingdom edn 1986 (Manchester, Manchester University Press)).

—— (1987) 'Sentencing by Numbers or Words?' in M Wasik and K Pease (eds), *Sentencing Reform: Guidance or Guidelines?* (Manchester, Manchester University Press).

—— (1989) 'Federal Sentencing Guidelines: Do They Provide Principled Guidance?' *American Criminal Law Review* 27, 367.

—— (1991) 'Criminal Record Rides Again' *Criminal Justice Ethics* 10, 2.

—— (1993) *Censure and Sanctions* (Oxford, Oxford University Press).

—— (1995) 'Proportionality and Parsimony in American Sentencing Guidelines: The Minnesota and Oregon Standards' in CMV Clarkson and R Morgan (eds), *The Politics of Sentencing Reform* (Oxford, Oxford University Press) 149, Ch 6.

—— (2001) *Proportionalitet och Straffbestämning* (Uppsala, Iustus Förlag).

—— (2001) 'Proportionate Sentencing for Juveniles: How Different than for Adults?' *Punishment & Society* 3, 221.

—— (2010) 'Proportionality and the Progressive Loss of Mitigation: Some Further Reflections' in A von Hirsch and JV Roberts (eds), *Previous Convictions at Sentencing: Theoretical and Applied Perspectives* (Oxford, Hart Publishing) Ch 1.

—— (2014) 'Harm and Wrongdoing in Criminalisation Theory' *Criminal Law & Philosophy* 8, 245.

von Hirsch, A and A Ashworth (2005) *Proportionate Sentencing: Exploring the Principles* (Oxford, Oxford University Press).

von Hirsch, A, A Ashworth, and JV Roberts (eds) (2009) *Principled Sentencing: Readings in Theory and Policy*, 3rd edn (Oxford, Hart Publishing).

von Hirsch, A, A Bottoms, et al (1999) Criminal Deterrence and Sentence Severity: An Analysis of Recent Research (Oxford, Hart Publishing).

von Hirsch, A and N Jareborg (1987), 'Straff och Proportionalitet' *Nordisk Tidsskrift for Kiminalvidenskab* 74, 56.

—— and —— (1989) 'Straff och Proportionalitet—Replik' *Nordisk Tidsskrift for Kiminalvidenskab* 76, 56.

—— and —— (1991) 'Gauging Criminal Harm: A Living-Standard Analysis' *Oxford Journal of Legal Studies* 11, 1.

von Hirsch, A and L Kazemian (2009) 'Predictive Sentencing and Selective Incapacitation' in A von Hirsch, A Ashworth and JV Roberts (eds) *Principled Sentencing: Readings in Theory and Policy* (Oxford, Hart Publishing) Ch 3.

von Hirsch, A, K Knapp and M Tonry (1987) *The Sentencing Commission and Its Guidelines* (Boston, Northeastern University Press).

Walker, Nigel (1991) *Why Punish?* (Oxford, Oxford University Press).

Ward, Tony and S Maruna (2007) *Rehabilitation* (London, Routledge).

Wasik, Martin (1987) 'Guidelines, Guidance and Criminal Record' in M Wasik and K Pease (eds), *Sentencing Reform: Guidance or Guidelines?* (Manchester, Manchester University Press) Ch 7.

Wasik, M and K Pease (eds) (1987) *Sentencing Reform: Guidance or Guidelines?* (Manchester, Manchester University Press).

Wasik, M and A von Hirsch (1988) 'Non-Custodial Penalties and the Principles of Desert' *Criminal Law Review* 555.

Wasserstrom, Richard (1980) *Philosophy and Social Issues: Five Studies* (Notre Dame, Indiana, University of Notre Dame Press).

Webster, Cheryl M and AN Doob (2012) 'Searching for Sasquatch: Deterrence of Crime through Sentence Severity' in J Petersilia and KR Reitz (eds), *The Oxford Handbook of Sentencing and Corrections* (New York, Oxford University Press).

Weijers, Ido and RA Duff (eds) (2002) *Punishing Juveniles: Principle and Critique* (Oxford, Hart Publishing).

White, Mark (ed) (2011) *Retributivism: Essays on Theory and Policy* (New York, Oxford University Press).

Williams, Bernard (1973) 'A Critique of Utilitarianism' in JJC Smart and B Williams (eds), *Utilitarianism: For and Against* (Cambridge, Cambridge University Press).

Wilson, James Q (1983) *Thinking about Crime*, revised edn (New York, Basic Books).

Windlesham, David (1996). *Responses to Crime.* New York: Oxford University Press, vol. 3.

Zedner, Lucia (1998) 'Sentencing Young Offenders' in A Ashworth and M Wasik (eds), *Fundamentals of Sentencing Theory: Essays in Honour of Andrew von Hirsch* (Oxford, Oxford University Press) Ch 7.

Zimring, Franklin E (1982) *The Changing Legal World of Adolescence* (New York, Free Press).

—— (1999) 'Toward a Jurisprudence of Youth Violence' in M Tonry and M Moore (eds), *Youth Violence. Criminal Justice: A Review of Research* (Chicago, Chicago University Press) Vol 24.

Zimring, Franklin E and G Hawkins (1995) *Incapacitation: Penal Confinement and the Restraint of Crime* (Oxford, Oxford University Press).

Zimring, Franklin E, G Hawkins and S Kamin (2001) *Punishment and Democracy: Three Strikes and You're Out in California* (New York, Oxford University Press).

Index

actor responsibility 33–4, 35
  see also moral agency
American Friends Service
  Committee 2
analytical moral philosophy 1–2
anchoring of penalty structure 22–3, 60–2
  guidance 62
  hypothetical scale 60–1
  moral claims 61–2
  see also cardinal proportionality;
    ordinal proportionality
Andenaes, J 47, 50
Ashworth, A 13, 43, 61, 124

Beccaria, C 46
Bentham, J 46, 109
bifurcated account *see under*
  punishment
blameworthy conduct 31–2
Bottoms, AE 90, 101–2, 103
breach sanction *see under* proportionate
  non-custodial sanctions
Brownsword, R 101–2, 103

cardinal proportionality
  anchoring *see* anchoring of penalty
    structure
  comparative blameworthiness 60
  imprecision of judgments 59
  ordinal proportionality,
    distinction 56, 60
  starting point 59–60
  see also ordinal proportionality
career-based system *see under* previous
  convictions
censure
  argument *see under* proportionate
    punishment's rationale
  and penal desert 17–20
    communicative features 17
    criminal sanction 17–18
    functions of censure 18
    hard treatment 19–20, 36–9
    role of proportionality 19
  role in punishment 32–5
chronology of model 143 *Appendix*

cognitive factors *see under* juvenile sentences
crime-control aims 25–7
  collateral benefits 26–7
  modified desert model 26
  ulterior aims 25–6
criminal sanction rationales
  bifurcated account *see under*
    punishment
  blameworthy conduct 31–2
  censure's role in punishment 32–5
  hard treatment *see* hard treatment
  theories *see* desert theories,
    varieties of
culpability 23

defiance argument *see under* previous
  convictions
deontological claims 41
derogation from proportionality 97
desert model
  ethical presuppositions 11–12
  evolution/chronology 143 *Appendix*
  meaning/main elements 1
  modifications *see* mixed models
  origins 1–4
  prevention *see* prevention-based
    sentencing
  proportionate sentence,
    attractions 7–8
  topics addressed 13–16
desert theories, varieties of 29–31
  broadest penal theory 29
  ordinary parlance 29
  requital for evil theory 29–30
  unfair advantage theory 30–1
Doing Justice: The Choice of Punishments
  (von Hirsch) 2, 143
Duff, A 42–3
Dworkin, R 99–100, 101*n*

England
  Criminal Justice Act 1991 119
  juvenile sentences 127
  proportionalism experience 3, 118–19
  Sentencing Guidelines Council
    3*n*, 16*n*, 127

ethical presuppositions 11–12
evolution/chronology of model
  143 *Appendix*
excuse doctrines 64

fairness 4, 7, 12
  proportionality 21
Feld, B 128
Finland
  proportionalism experience
    6–7, 117, 118
  underlying social ills 123

Gardner, M 124
Germany, juvenile sentences 127
guidance/guidelines for
  sentencing 15–16
  seriousness comparison 63

hard treatment
  censure 36
  and penal desert 19–20, 36–9
  preventative process 36–7
  prudential disincentive 37–8
  see also criminal sanction
    rationales
Howard, Michael 119, 120
human nature 38
hybrid models *see* mixed models

incapacitation, selective 10
intentional conduct/negligence
  distinction 64
Israel, proportionalism
  experience 3, 118

Jareborg, N 64, 65, 73
justice, primacy of 12
juvenile sentences
  cognitive factors 130–3
    age-based gradations 132–3
    awareness of others'
      interests 130–1
    descriptive approach 132
    normative expectations 131–2
  culpability arguments 129
  European approaches 127
  individual assessment 134–5
  key issues/conclusion 15, 128–9, 141
  punitive bite 135–7
    developmental interests 136
    interests-analysis 136–7
    self-esteem capacity 136–7
    subjectivist view 135–6

special tolerance 137–41
  availability 141
  bad choices risk 140–1
  consequentialist concerns 139
  cutting losses response 138–9
  experimentation process 138
  first-offender discount 76–7, 140
  key issues 137–8
  retrospective criteria 139–40
  temporary nature 141
volitional controls 133–4
youth discount 134

Kahan, D 110
Kant, I 38, 41
Kleinig, J 2

Lacey, N 125
law and order strategies 110, 118–21
  aim 120–1
  as communicative punishment 121
  populist punitiveness 120
  proliferation 118–19
Lee, Y 85
limiting retributivism 55–6, 103–4
living-standard
  concept 24, 64–7
  levels 66
  punishment severity 69, 125–6

Minnesota guidelines 90, 116
  see also US Sentencing Commission,
    Guidelines
mixed models
  alternative penalties 97
  Bottoms–Brownsword model
    101–2, 103
  conclusions 105–6
  derogation from proportionality 97
  individual dangerousness
    standard 101–2
  limiting retributivism 55–6, 103–4
  modified desert model
    non-custodial penalties
      scaling 105
    restricted deviations 104
    specified limits 104–5
    ulterior ends identified 105, 106
  other desired ends 97
  ranges of punishment 103–5
  Robinson's model 98–101, 103
    absolute/important constraint,
      distinction 100–1
    fairness constraints 100

harm prevention 101
overriding grounds 99–100
quarantine parallel 98–9
upward deviations 98
tentativeness 98
see also desert model
moral accountability 33
moral agency 12, 38–9, 109
see also actor responsibility
Morris, N 55–6, 57, 58, 62, 103, 104

non-custodial sanctions *see* proportionate
non-custodial sanctions
Nordic countries
experience 116–18
writings 108

ordinal proportionality
anchoring *see* anchoring of penalty
structure
and broad limits 57
cardinal proportionality,
distinction 56, 60
concept/requirements 56–7
crime prevention concerns 58–9
meaning 13, 22–3
parity *see* parity requirement
rank-ordering 58
see also cardinal proportionality
Oregon 90*n*, 118

parity requirement
ordinal proportionality 58
substitutions among penalties 89–90
penal utilitarianism 35, 111–15
deterrence argument 46–7, 112–13
harshness/moderation
possibilities 111
indeterminacy risk 111
intermediate sanctions 115
preventative efficacy 112–13
rehabilitation 112, 113–15
selective incapacitation 113
penalties
anchoring *see* anchoring of penalty
structure
substitutions *see under* proportionate non-
custodial sanctions
penance model 42–3
Pickard, H 125
political arguments
conservative penal theorists 110–11
desert model responses 108–9
key issues 15, 107

law and order *see* law and order
strategies
neo-classicist label 109
Nordic writings 108
proportionalism and increased severity,
argument 115–18
retributivism considered
reactionary 107
utilitarianism *see* penal utilitarianism
vacuousness argument 125–6
positive general prevention 34–5
preventative efficacy *see under* penal utilitarianism
prevention-based sentencing 8–11
fairness deficit 11
general deterrence 9–10
marginal effects 9, 10
rehabilitation 9
selective incapacitation 10
severity effects 10
previous convictions
activity diminishing with age 81–2
career-based system 74–5
criminal/non-criminal regulation,
comparison 80–1
current conduct arguments 73
defiance argument 73
desert rationales 72
desistance issue 79–80
ignorance/inattention argument 73–4
key issues/conclusion 14, 72, 85
multiple offending 79–80
number of 84
opinions' divergence 85
prediction studies 71–2
progressive-loss-of-mitigation
model 72, 79, 82–3, 85
selective entry criteria 80
seriousness of 84
tolerance *see* tolerance and prior record
weight question 71
progressive-loss-of-mitigation
model 72, 79, 82–3, 85
proportionality of sentence
attractions 7–8
censure *see* censure, and penal desert
crime-control *see* crime-control aims
culpability 23
increased severity argument 115–18
limiting/determining principle,
distinction 21–3
living-standard idea 24
ordinal proportionality 22–3
penal severity question 27

previous convictions   24–5
rationale   20–1
retrospective principle   21
seriousness of crime and severity of
    punishment   23–4
proportionate non-custodial sanctions
advantages   88–9
background   87
breach sanction   93–5
    components of breach   94
    incarceration reliance   93
    modest penalty increase   94–5
    reoffending sanctions   95
imprisonment restriction   88
intermediate sanctions,
    restrictions   88
key elements/conclusion
    14, 87–8, 94–5
revocation sanction   88
scale of punishments,
    simplicity   88
substitutions among penalties
    88, 89–93
    approximate equivalence   89
    crime prevention concerns   89–90
    degrees of substitutability   91–2
    full-substitution   92
    hard/sharp demarcation   90–1
    limited substitutability   92–3
    numerical sentencing
        guidelines   90
    parity *see* parity requirement
proportionate punishment's rationale
background   13, 45
censure argument
    basic argument   49–50
    circularity question   50
    and preventative grounds   52–4
    schematic steps   51
deterrence argument   46–7
ethical principle   48
positive general prevention   47–8
preventative grounds   52–4
prudential disincentive   40, 53
punishment
bifurcated account   37–8
    hypothetical abolition   42
    penance model   42–3
    prevention and censure   40–1, 52–4
    proportionality requirement   39
    relative/absolutist dichotomy   41
    state's role   41–2, 43
blameworthy conduct   31–2
censure's role   32–5

hard treatment *see* hard treatment
penance model   42–3
severity *see under* seriousness gauging
Punishment and Desert (Kleinig)   2
punishment severity *see* severity of
    punishments
punitive bite *see under* juvenile sentences

rank-ordering *see under* ordinal
    proportionality
rehabilitation   9
    penal utilitarianism   112, 113–15
    prevention-based sentencing   9
    and tolerance and prior record   78–9
requital for evil theory   29–30
retributive notions
    limiting retributivism   55–6
    objections to   4
Roberts, JV   85
Robinson's model *see under* mixed models
rule of law   12

sanction severity *see* severity of
    punishments
Scotland, juvenile sentences   127
selective incapacitation   10
self-control *see* juvenile sentences,
    volitional controls
Sen, A   64–5, 125–6
Sentencing Guidelines Council
    (England)   3*n*, 16*n*, 127
seriousness gauging   14, 63–7, 125–6
    consensus   63
    criteria   64
    guidelines *see* guidance/guidelines for
        sentencing
    guidelines commissions   63
    harm analysis   64–7
    severity of punishments
        assessment ability   67
        interests-analysis   68–9
        opinion surveys   67–8
        subjectivist approach   68
severity of punishments *see under*
    seriousness gauging
special tolerance *see under* juvenile
    sentences
Spielraumtheorie   103
standard of living *see* living-standard
state responsibility   12
Straw, Jack   119, 120
Strawson, PF   33
Struggle for Justice (American Friends Service
    Committee)   2

substitutions among penalties
see under proportionate
non-custodial sanctions
Sweden
juvenile sentences   127
reoffending treatment
and desistance   83
middle range of seriousness   82–3
penal interventions, limited
reliance   83
proportionalism experience   82–3,
117, 118
sentencing scheme
Finnish law influence   6–7
limited substitutability   92–3
reform provisions   5–6
treatment-based sentences   4–5
underlying social ills   123
Swedish Penal Code   5, 6, 7

talionic notions   4, 8, 109
third party desistance   34
tolerance and prior record   75–9
and career-desert perspective   78
first-offender discount   76–7, 140
human fallibility   75–6
lapse notion   76
and rehabilitation   78–9
repetitions of offences   77

underlying social ills   122–5
conservative utilitarian theories   122
continuing presence of crime   122–3
disadvantaged offenders   123–4
as extenuating circumstances   124
poverty-based mitigation   125
United Kingdom *see* England
US Sentencing Commission,
Guidelines   115–16
see also Minnesota guidelines
utilitarianism *see* penal utilitarianism

vacuousness argument   125–6
van den Haag, E   110
victimising offences   65–6
volitional controls *see under* juvenile
sentences

Wasik-von Hirsch model
see proportionate non-custodial
sanctions
Wasserstrom, R   31
wellbeing concept   64–5
Wilson, JQ   110

youth discount *see under* juvenile
sentences

Zimring, FE   128, 138, 141